Chinese Court Judgements

Intellectual Property

Chinese Court Judgements

Intellectual Property

Fei Ming

Legend Business, 2 London Wall Buildings,
London EC2M 5UU
business@legend-paperbooks.co.uk
www.legendpress.co.uk

Contents © Fei Ming 2011

The right of the above author to be identified as the author of this work has been asserted in accordance with the Copyright, Designs and Patent Act 1988.

British Library Cataloguing in Publication Data available.

ISBN 978-1-9074612-0-0

Set in Times
Printed by Lightning Source, Milton Keynes.

All rights reserved. No part of this publication may be reproduced, stored in or introduced into a retrieval system, or transmitted, in any form, or by any means electronic, mechanical, photocopying, recording or otherwise, without the prior permission of the publisher. Any person who commits any unauthorised act in relation to this publication may be liable to criminal prosecution and civil claims for damages.

DISCLAIMER

The publishers and author have taken all reasonable care in the preparation of this book but cannot accept responsibility for the complete accuracy of the texts which are edited translations into English from the original transcripts in Chinese.

For more information:

www.chinesecourtjudgements.com

About the Author

The author Lawyer Fei Ming holds a Master's Degree in Law from the University of New South Wales, Australia. As a professional lawyer in China, he has long served as attorney for foreign clients on matters of intellectual property protection in China, and possesses rich practical legal experience.

Lawyer Fei Ming's E-mail: **findchinalawyer.fei@gmail.com**
Personal Website: **www.findchinalawyer.com**

Table of contents

For the convenience of readers, page references for each judgement are listed under one of six columns identifying the nature of the dispute, as follows:

"A" identifies cases described by the Court as Trade Infringements.
"B" identifies cases listed as Brand Disputes.
"C" identifies cases listed as Copyright Infringements.
"D" identifies cases relating to distribution or "information dissemination", including Internet downloads.
"E" identifies cases listed as Patent Disputes.
"F" identifies cases involving claims of counterfeiting, unfair competition or breach of confidentiality.

	A	B	C	D	E	F/G
Part One – 2008-2009						
1. Niu Xiaolong Vs CAJEPH			25			
2. Pan Jiangli Vs Wenzhou Calendar, Cangnan County Zongwen, Huang Zongwen & He Hui				27		
3. Hebei Henshui Wine Stock Vs Hengshui Henglong Laobaigan Wine			28			
4. Puma Aktengesellshaft Rudolf Dessler Sport vs Fuqing City Left-coast Bali Mal		30				
5. Wuhan Yongning Building Materials Vs Hubei Zhujin Fangshui Engineering		31				
6. Hsin Weng Chan Vs Cheng Bin & Estate Company of Wuhan Decoration Material Square		32				

	A	B	C	D	E	F/G
7. Beijing Netmovie Company Vs Wuhan Explorer Computer Serving				34		
8. Beijing Three Facing Copyright Agency Vs Jiangxi Xingxi Education Live and Jiangxi Xingxi Education Software			35			
9. Wuhan Haier Refrigerator Vs Dai Shaoshun					36	
10. Shanghai Hongqi Yonghe Food Devt. Stock Vs Qiao Hongxia		38				
11. Jinan Wode Automobile Parts Vs Shanghai Xuntai Industry & Trade		39				
12. Beijing Quanjing Shituo Pictures Vs Fuzhou Daily News & Tianjin Zhongxin Pharmaceutical Group			40			
13. Guangdong Suihong Culture Development Vs Chongqing High Tech District New Green Net Bar Yuying				41		
14. Beijing Tianyu Tongsheng Information Technology Vs Chongqing Yubei Green Boat Karaoke			42			
15. Bejing Rongxinda Films & TV Vs ChinaTelecom Stock, Hebei Branch				43		
16. Center Music (Shenzhen) Vs Chongqing Yubei Green Boat Music Building				44		
17. Center Music Company (Shenzhen) Vs Shanghai Xianzi Entertainment				45		
18. Cartier International NV Vs Hubei Tongtian Hotel		46				
19. Honda Motor Co Vs Beian Century Economy Trade		47				
20. Taishan Plasterboard Stock Vs Tu Yonghua		48				

	A	B	C	D	E	F/G
21. People's Court Publishing House & Beijing Wanguo Fayuan Education Technology Vs Niu Zhenshui			49			
22. Shanghai Yingge Import & Export Vs Wang Xiuping						50
23. Yuan Kai Yin Vs Liuu Yunhua					52	
24. Hu Wuyi Vs Yeyun & Yongkang City Building Tool Company					53	
25. Kong Lingsuo Vs Shanghai Jingdun Fire Controlling Safety Equipment					54	
26. Liu Wangyan Vs Chongqing Times Agency			55			
27. Shanghai Naikai Electrics Vs Shanghai Yuanbai Information Technology, Shanghai Yuanli Numerical Control Machines & Shanghai Zhongtang Electrics Technology			56			
28. Guozi Film Vs China Telecom Stock & Wuhan Changjiang Mutual Media				58		
29. Wangyu Vs China TieTong Group Gao Linjun				59		
30. Chongqing Zongshen Technology Development Vs Chongqing Yongsheng Die-casting					60	
31. Lu Futong Vs Shenzhen Hengfa Daily Texture & Walmart Eastern					61	
32. Zhangzhe Supor Stock Vs Lian Qiaomei& Zhou Chunqiu			62			
33. Shanghai Shikumen Brewing Vs Shaoxing Yuegong Brewing, Shanghai Tinglian & Jieqiangyingxiang Supermarket of Shanghai Wangrong Industrial & Trade					63	

	A	B	C	D	E	F/G
34. Shanghai Lingke Technology Vs Shanghai Juxin Automatic Technology			65			
35. WLNET (Beijing) Technology Vs Shanghai Gaochin Communication Technology				66		
36. Ningbo Success Media Communication Vs Shanghai VC Network Technology				68		
37. Getty Images China Vs Chongqing Hotel			69			
38. Guangdong Panda Daily Chemical Products Vs Wang Hande		70				
39. Beijing Three-Oriented Copyright Agency Vs Pinxiang City Campus of Jiangxi Radio and Television University			71			
40. Wang Peng Vs Shanghai Han Ni Di Restaurant Management		73				
41. Guangzhou Daming United Rubber Products Vs Chongqing Jiu-Kang Medical Instrument		74				
42. Beijing Kinmen and Matsu Culture Communication Vs Wuhan Lu Di Bear Music Entertainment			75			
43. Shanghai High Mountains and Long River Garments Vs Yan Dalun & Feng Dawei			76			
44. Aerfenna Electrical Systems Vs Zhejiang Lido Electric					77	
45. Taiwan D-Link Electronic Equipment (Shanghai) Vs Lai Changhua		78				
46. He Haiqun Vs Municipal Library of Wenzhou			79			

	A	B	C	D	E	F/G

47. Zhong Zhiwen Vs Yueqing
    Tiang Mei Tools ... 80
48. Yanghe Brewery Vs Heyang
    Brewery & Shanghai Xinchen
    Trade ... 81

Part Two – 2004 – 2007
49. Xingyuan & Starbucks Coffee
    Vs Shanghai Starbucks &
    Shanghai Starbucks & Shanghai
    Starbuck Branch ... 85
50. The Extra-budgetary Fund
    Administrative Bureau of
    Guannan County & Liangxinaghe
    Vs Tao Qin ... 86
51. Jinan Ward Auto Parts Vs Wei
    Changjun ... 88
52. Bonneterie Cévenole Vs
    Shanghai Meizheng ... 89
53. Guoxing Tendering Vs Beijing
    Bidcenter Information Technology ... 90
54. Brilliance Jinbei Vs Jin Cheng ... 91
55. Music Copyright Society of China Vs
    Shenzhen Konka Telecommunications
    Technology & Beijing Tongwanbao
    Commercial and Trade ... 92
56. Hong Qingqi Vs National Palace
    Museum, Beijing Ideal Creative
    Art Design ... 94
57. Jinag Tao Vs Xidian University
    Press ... 95
58. AgrEvo Vs Nanjing First Pesticide
    Plant ... 96
59. Kohler Vs Beijing Meilian Tiandi
    Material Mart ... 97

	A	B	C	D	E	F/G
60. Danfoss Vs Zibo-based Danfosi Detection & Control Instrument	99					
61. Cui Shixun Vs Lianong Provincial Library						101
62. Eastman Kodak Vs Keda Elevator	102					

Part Three 1998 – 2003

	A	B	C	D	E	F/G
63. Autodesk Vs Longfa			105			
64. (America) Education Testing Center (ETS) Vs New Oriental School			106			
65. America Adobe Vs Shanghai Nianhua Computer Videotext Technology			107			
66. Laolishi Vs Beijing Cinet Information		108				
67. Lek-Yuen Vs Jinlanwan						109
68. Tianjin Quanxing Sporting Products Factory Vs Sichuan Quanxing Football Club & Nanjing Sport Equipment Factory	110					
69. Suzuki Motor Vs San Li	111					
70. Lin Yi ChinaNews Agency			113			
71. Beijing Finance City Network Vs Chengdu Moneywise Software						114
72. Xinhai Advertising Vs Chengdu Economic TV Station			115			
73. Jiang Haixin vs Philips	116					
74. Music Copyright Society of China Vs Netease.com & China Mobil			117			
75. Japanese Yamaha Vs South Motorcycle & Gangtian	118					

	A	B	C	D	E	F/G
76. Xuzhou Handu Industrial Development Vs Japanese Olympus Optical Industry	119					
77. Dupont Vs Beijing Guowang Information	120					
78. Inter Ikea Systems Vs Guowang Information	121					
79. Zhao Jikang Vs Qujing Cigarette Factory						122
80. Anhui Xiaoxiao Technology Industrial Vs Jixi County Light Chain Factory						123

FOREWORD

Intellectual property protection in China is a relatively new phenomenon. There is no cultural tradition of respect for the intellectual property rights (IPR) of others. Chinese inventiveness and art through the ages has evolved as strongly as in the Western world but without inhibitions on copying the work of other people. Far from regarding the reproduction without consent of patented designs, prior art, brands or published work under copyright as theft or plagiarism, the Chinese have followed the Confucian preference for 'transmission rather than creation' with the attitude that copying others' ideas is a form of positive compliment – a reflection perhaps of the Oscar Wilde aphorism that 'imitation is the sincerest form of flattery'.

Although Western concepts of IPR were introduced to China in the first half of the 20th century and more particularly since the adoption of Deng Xiaoping's 'open door' policy in 1979, the protection of IPR has remained a major concern for all foreign companies seeking to invest, transfer technology or market their branded products. Following World Trade Organization (WTO) entry Chinese enterprises have been under close scrutiny and suffered sanctions for their use of others' IPR; however, only since 2008, when the State Council issued the Outline of National IPR Strategy accompanied by a series of measures and amendments to previous IPR laws in China, have Western investors and trading partners gained confidence that there is a manageable patent and trademark system that offers proper protection.

The reasons for China's new understanding and respect are threefold. First, it is well recognized that firm IPR protection is a prerequisite for much foreign direct investment; second, China needs protection for its own intellectual property in global economic activity. Third, and by no means the least significant, Chinese enterprises in the coastal provinces and their hinterlands now face IPR infringement daily from new businesses in the previously undeveloped provinces as economic prosperity and manufacturing activity spreads eastwards.

Education is playing an important part in changing attitudes and understanding, driven by forward-looking provincial and city governments. As early as 1986 Renmin University in Beijing established the first intellectual property teaching centre in China, followed in the same year by Huazhong University of Science and Technology in Wuhan, and in 1993 by Beijing University with its own Intellectual Property School. Eight universities in the Shanghai area have developed a specialism in intellectual property under the Shanghai Intellectual Property Administration (SIPA). Perhaps the most striking example of how intellectual property awareness is being introduced in both primary, junior middle and senior middle school is the Foshan initiative under the leadership of its mayor to generate respect and awareness among teenagers of the need to protect intellectual property.

However, it will be some time before these initiatives achieve a fundamental change in culture. Meantime, the sympathetic public attitude to IPR infringement makes enforcement hard work, particularly in the case of factories producing counterfeit goods which alleviate poverty by providing employment.

Nevertheless, the various levels of Chinese Courts are doing their best to interpret and apply intellectual property law. This book offers a compilation of Court judgements given between 1998 and 2009 on a range of intellectual property issues. Together, they provide a flavour of the evolution in Court judgements in cases of intellectual property, some of which Western practitioners in IPR may find at variance with Western practice. IPR protection and litigation in China continues to evolve, but these judgements are valuable practical evidence of the outcomes that foreign companies doing business in China may expect in IPR disputes. To illustrate the change in Court attitudes to IPR violation, the later sections of these reports include a selection of Senior Court past judgements from earlier years dating back to 1998 which show how China's treatment of IPR violations has matured. I recommend this book to corporate lawyers, IPR practitioners and senior business management as an important source of reference.

Jonathan Reuvid
London, 2011

INTRODUCTION

If you have businesses or have made investment in China, you will have to consider whether your intellectual property, business secrets and other valuable properties can be fully protected by the law in China.

It is widely known that China is an emerging market with tremendous growth potential. However, China still has much to do when it comes to intellectual property protection. In China, your computer software may be widely pirated, as Microsoft has experienced. Your garment brand may also be brought into an awkward situation by local fake goods at extremely low prices, as Louis Vuitton has been. Your trademark, patent, music or works may be freely used, without fees paid to you. In the end, you may have no choice other than to resort to the protection of Chinese laws.

How then do Chinese laws protect intellectual property? What special provisions are there? Perhaps different from what is generally known, China has adopted a civil law system. All its intellectual property laws are dispersed between such written laws as the criminal law, the civil law, the contract law and various other procedure laws. However, it is obvious that you can hardly be expected to understand such a broad array of Chinese legal provisions.

In this book we have collected, sorted out and extracted 80 typical cases which People's Courts at various levels in China heard from 1998 to 2009. These cases involve the Internet, trademarks, copyright, patent right, audio and video works, food and various other aspects. The book provides a summary reference guide for fast reading and will save corporate managers all the trouble of studying China's various legal provisions in the way that experts do. If your intellectual property happens to be infringed in China, you can refer to this book and imagine, in a self-help manner, how a Chinese Court would protect your interests. Meanwhile, experts and scholars can also learn from this book the general history and development trend of China's intellectual property laws.

The book is organized in three parts: Part One includes selected Court judgements for the most recent years 2008 and 2009; Part Two covers the three-year period 2004 to 2007; and Part Three cases are across the period 1998 to 2003. In Parts two and Three, we have included as many cases as possible involving well-know Western companies. For the convenience of readers wishing to focus on their own situations we have added a Table of Contents, which identifies by case number the main types of intellectual property dispute.

From this book, you can gain some general idea about how Chinese Courts protect intellectual property. Moreover, you will also gain some idea about the outlook for your intellectual property in China.

Fei Ming
Beijing, 2011

CHINESE COURT JUDGEMENTS: INTELLECTUAL PROPERTY

PART ONE: 2008 - 2009

CASE NO. 1

Niu Xiaolong Vs. CAJEPH
2008
First People's Court in Haidian, Beijing City

COPYRIGHT DISPUTE
The Plaintiff is the author of an academic thesis "Shang". He has given an authorization to Anhui University, of which the essence is that the university reserves rights to keep copies of the thesis, and is allowed to permit others to read it. The university can compile parts or the whole content into its database for indexing, and can also use photocopying, reduction printing and other copying methods to keep or compile the thesis. On April 28, 2008, the Graduate Department of Anhui University authorized a certain magazine agency to use certain theses including "Shang" in its electronic magazine and database of academic theses titled "Data Base for Excellent Chinese Graduate Theses" on www.cnki.com, where Plaintiff's thesis can be accessed.

HELD: When the Plaintiff submitted his thesis for an academic degree awarded by Anhui University, he authorized the university to compile part or all of the thesis into its database for indexing, and to use photocopying, reduction printing and other copying methods to keep or compile the thesis. Based on this authorization, the university then published and propagated "Shang" by way of compiling it into databases that were outside the range of its authorization. The letter of authorization did not indicate whether the university that awarded the academic degree could make such re-authorizations, and the university is not an enterprise engaged in the publishing and propagation of written works. However, the university published and propagated "Shang" generally by giving authorizations to other parties. Specifically, the university authorized the magazine agency to compile the "Shang" thesis into its graduate thesis database. Then the magazine agency authorized Tongfang Company to use "Shang" in its publication, and it was lawful for the magazine agency and Tongfang company to exploit the thesis. Therefore, there is no legal evidence for the Plaintiff to demand that the magazine agency and Tongfang Company bear any responsibility for copyright infringement.

CASE NO. 2

Pan Jiangli Vs. Wenzhou Xinlian Calendar Ltd, Cangnan County Zongwen Ltd, Huang Zongwen and He Hui
2009
Intermediate People's Court of Hengshui City, Hebei Province

COPYRIGHT & PROPERTY DISPUTE
The Plaintiff is the owner of copyright for three sets of paper-cut tiger dolls. The Defendant, Cangnan County Zongwen Calendar Ltd sells the three sets of paper-cut tiger dolls to the public through its website. The relevant paper-cut works manufactured by the Defendant He Hui were provided by Wenzhou Xinlian Calendar Ltd.

HELD: The three relevant sets of paper-cut products were originated by the Plaintiff who holds the protection of copyright law for all three sets. The Defendants Wenzhou Xinlian Calendar Ltd, Cangnan County Zongwen Calendar Ltd and Huang Zongwen used the relevant three sets of paper-cut products without the Plaintiff's permission, and their actions constitute copyright infringement. Regarding the amount of compensation, the court will take the following factors into comprehensive consideration: the Plaintiff's reputation, reasonable use of the products, the degree and nature of copyright infringement, the quantities of the relevant three sets of paper-cut products sold by the three defendants and the reasonable fees paid by the Plaintiff to prosecute his case, to determine the exact amounts of compensation. The Defendant He Hui who produced the infringing products should bear the legal responsibility of ceasing manufacture; however, he was unaware of the infringement and has also provided evidence proving that the works were furnished by the other three Defendants. Therefore, He Hui does not bear responsibility for compensation.

CASE NO. 3

Hebei Hengshui Laobaigan Wine Stock Ltd Vs. Hengshui Henglong Laobaigan Wine Ltd
2009
Intermediate People's Court of Hengshui City, Hebei Province

DISPUTE REGARDING THE ILLEGAL USE OF THE BRAND NAME, PACKAGING AND DECORATION OF FAMOUS GOODS

The inner and outer packaging of Hengshui (henglong) Laobaigan 67 degree, 55 degree, 50 degree and 45 degree frosted-bottle white wine produced by the Defendant is very similar to the goods of the Plaintiff.

HELD: "Hengshui Laobaigan" is both the registered trademark and company name of the Plaintiff. At the same time, it's a proprietary name for the Plaintiff's products. Hengshui (henglong) Laobaigan 67 degree, 50 degree with five years' ageing, 45 degree frosted-bottle white wine is produced by the defendant using the " Hengshui Laobaigan" trademark, with the same size of characters as the Plaintiff's, but inserting the letter characters of "henglong" between "heng" and "shui" or between "hengshui" and "laobaigan". The actions of the Defendant infringed the Plaintiff's proprietary names for its famous goods. White wine bottle cases for Hengshui (henglong) Laobaigan 67 degree, 55 degree and 50 degree with five years' ageing, use the same or similar pictures to the Plaintiff's Hengshui Laobaigan 67 degree, 55 degree and 42 degree with three years' ageing respectively; the arrangement of characters and pictures of the ranges of products are identical. The wine bottles and labels for the Defendant's 50 degree with five years' ageing and 45 degree frosted-bottle white wine are the same or similar to the Plaintiff's 42 degree with three years' ageing and 42 degree frosted-bottle white wine. The Defendant's four relevant kinds of goods infringed the proprietary packaging and decoration of the products belonging to the Plaintiff.

The actions of the defendant can mislead consumers, making them believe that the Defendant's products originate from the Plaintiff and therefore constitute illegal competition.

CASE NO. 4

Puma Aktiengesellschaft Rudolf Dassler Sport Vs. Fuqing City Left-coast Bali Mall Ltd
2008
Intermediate People's Court of Fuzhou City

EXCLUSIVE TRADEMARK RIGHTS DISPUTE
The Plaintiff is the owner of the trademark; the Defendant sells products with the trademark attached without the permission of the Plaintiff.

HELD: English language characters and the combination of pictures of socks from the Defendant are identical to the those of the Plaintiff, the shape of the characters is also the same, the whole shape of the pictures are similar and the two designs are very similar to each other. Therefore, without any visible difference, they are recognized as the same trademark. The Defendant sells products with the trademark attached, and without the agreement of the Plaintiff the action is a trademark infringement. Nor did the Defendant provide the legal origin of the products and should bear responsibility for ceasing the infringement and compensating the Plaintiff for loss. Because neither the Plaintiff nor the Defendant provided evidence of the benefits and losses due to infringement, the Court should take into account comprehensively the popularity of the trademark, the nature, period and results of the infringement, to arrive at the amount of compensation.

CASE NO. 5

Wuhan Yongning Building Materials Ltd Vs. Hubei Zhujin Fangshui Engineering Ltd
2009
Intermediate People's Court of Wuhan City Hubei Province

COPYRIGHT DISPUTE

The Plaintiff, with the benefit of copyright, reserves the right to own, use and edit the relevant photograph. The Defendant used the photograph in its promotional leaflet without authorization.

HELD: The name of the photograph used by the Defendant is "Sewage Treatment Plant Water-proof in Wuhan South Prince Lake" and is the same as the Plaintiff's photograph named "Sewage Treatment Plant in Wuhan South Prince Lake" in respect of photographic character, composition, angle, scene, shadow, action, activity and inertia, and the position of the objects in the photograph. Therefore, it can be recognized that the picture used in The Defendant's promotional leaflet is taken from the Plaintiff's photograph. The Defendant has no evidence to prove that it acquired permission from the Plaintiff to use the relevant photograph in its promotional leaflet. Therefore, the action of the Defendant infringed the Plaintiff's copyright.

CASE NO. 6

Hsin Wen Chang vs. Cheng Bin and Estate Company of Wuhan Yijia Decoration Material Square.
2009
Intermediate People's Court of Wuhan City Hubei Province

EXCLUSIVE REGISTERED TRADEMARK RIGHT DISPUTE
The Plaintiff legally holds the trademark together with images and characters. His exclusive trademark right is valid until May 6, 2011. The Defendant Chen Bin signed a one year shop lease as a tenant for the period from March 2003 to February 2004 with Wuhan Xinya Economic and Development Ltd. The place of business was 6F2-B20 Yijia Decoration Square Xiaodongmen, Wu Chang, Wuhan. As a tenant, The Defendant Chen Bin went on to sign a shop lease with the defendant Yijia Estate Company in respect of the same place of business as above for the period March 2004 to February 2009. At the relevant site consisting of one store on two floors in Yijia Decoration Square Xiaodongmen, Wu Chang, Wuhan, there is a hanging sign saying "Canada DSH Cabinet" with a DSH picture. In his promotional leaflet the Defendant Cheng Bin shows the company name "Wuhan City Xinxiang Decoration Material Ltd" on the cover page, identified by the DSH logo with pictures of the products. The last page features a "customized cabinet illustration" with a guarantee certificate and includes the DSH logo and words "DSH cabinet". On the inner pages of the promotional leaflet, there are product pictures, all with the DSH logo. In addition, the place of business is identified as Wuchang Specialty Store, i.e. 6F2-B20 Yijia Decoration Square Xiaodongmen.

HELD: As a distributor of home decoration and building products, the Defendant Cheng Bin has an overriding responsibility to check trademarks in this field. Trademarks possess high recognition in decoration materials. The Defendant Cheng Bin should be aware of the DSH trademark, and has a responsibility to avoid infringing the exclusive rights of the trademark. Without permission from the Plaintiff, Cheng Bin hung a sign saying "Canada DSH Cabinet" with the DSH logo; he also identified pictures of his products with the DSH logo. His actions at first sight imply a sales promise, but in fact he uses the DSH characters and logo to promote his own products, which will readily give the impression that his products are related to the products of the Plaintiff, thereby confusing consumers as to the origin of the products and with the deliberate intention of passing them off as genuine DSH products. Analyzing his product range, the defendant Cheng Bin specializes in house decoration and building materials. According to the characteristics of the operation, Cheng Bin specializes in manufacturing and selling home decoration and building materials to customized designs and sizes as requested by customers. After finishing manufacture, he assembles the products ordered by customers for the purpose of sale. Based on popularity and confidence in "DSH" cabinets, when consumers saw the hung business plate saying "Canada DSH Cabinet", they were misled into believing that products of Cheng Bin had some relation to the famous DSH brand, and they then purchased products from Cheng Bin. The Defendant Cheng Bin manufactured and sold infringing products and used a similar logo to that of Hsin Weng Chang, which also constitutes an infringement, and Cheng Bin should bear corresponding responsibility for compensation. The Defendant Yijia Estate Company rented the shop located in Yijia Square Xiaodongmen in Wuhan to Defendant Cheng Bin for business, authorized by people not involved in this case. The Plaintiff has no evidence proving that this Defendant had any interest in the business of Cheng Bin, and no evidence to prove that the Defendants Yijia Estate Company and Cheng Bin collaborated to practice the infringement. When Hsin Wen Chang first filed its prosecution in 2008, Defendant Yijia Estate Company urged Defendant Cheng Bin to remove the plate inscribed with "Canada DSH Cabinet". Therefore, Defendant Yijia Estate Company should bear no responsibility. Cheng Bin is an independent licensed business entity. He is responsible for the infringement in his business operation and the legal consequences should be borne by him. The Plaintiff's claim that Yijia Estate Company and Cheng Bin combined to commit the infringement, and request that Yijia Estate Company should bear responsibility for the relevant civil compensation arising from Defendant Cheng Bin's infringement is rejected.

CASE NO. 7

Beijing Netmovie Company Ltd Vs. Wuhan Explorer Computer Serving Ltd
2009
Intermediate People's Court of Wuhan City Hubei Province

RIGHTS TO NETWORK DISSEMINATION OF CONTENT
The Plaintiff owns exclusively copyright over the four following titles: *Criminal Intelligence Bureau*, *At Home With Love*, *Face To Fate* and *Forensic Heroes*. The copyright includes but is not limited to internal information dissemination rights, copying rights and performance rights in the People's Republic of China. The Defendant provided all four titles to clients for live viewing through the local area network without the permission of the copyright owner.

HELD: TVB Company is the original copyright owner of *Criminal Intelligence Bureau*, *At Home With Love*, *Face To Fate* and *Forensic Heroes*. The Plaintiff Beijing Netmovie Company has the rights to network distribution in mainland China authorized by TVB Company. The authorization covers exclusive performance rights and resale rights and precludes infringement. Thus the Plaintiff owns legal and effective authorization, and should be protected by the Law.

CASE NO. 8

Beijing Three Facing Copyright Agency Company Vs. Jianxi Xingzhi Education Live Ltd and Jiangxi Xingzhi Education Software Ltd.
2009
Higher People's Court of Jiangxi Province

COPYRIGHT INFRINGEMENT DISPUTE
The Plaintiff owns copyright for *Xiaohunyizhiling*. The Defendant broadcast the work on the Internet without permission.

HELD: The Plaintiff acquired the relevant copyright except for signature and revision rights through a copyright assignment contract, which should be protected by Law. The Defendants broadcast *Xiaohunyizhiling* on their own website, thereby violating the Plaintiff's right to network dissemination of information and its right to reserve the related benefits.

CASE NO. 9

Wuhan Haier Refrigerator Ltd Vs. Dai Shaochun
2009
Intermediate People's Court of Wuhan City Hubei Province

PATENT RIGHTS OWNERSHIP DISPUTE
The Defendant Dai Shaochun is an employee of the Plaintiff, working mainly on welding, to improve welding quality and train welders. The Defendant Dai Shaochun took the lead in providing a proposal for the improvement of a folding door hinge of a horizontal refrigerator. He made a rough draft which he sent by e-mail to his employer, Wuhan Haier Refrigerator Ltd. On March 6, 2008, the two parties severed their labor relations, the Defendant left the company on that day and the handover work list to his superior at the Plaintiff included an improvement proposal for the folding door hinge of a horizontal refrigerator. On November 10, 2008, the two parties signed a Patent Application Transfer Agreement, stipulating transfer of the patent application to Wuhan Haier Refrigerator Ltd. After signing the agreement, the Plaintiff applied to the State Intellectual Property Office to change the registration. Subsequently, Defendant Dai Shaochun filed an objection so that the registration change was aborted.

HELD: There was a labor relationship between the Plaintiff and the Defendant, with whom there was a valid labor contract from March 6, 2007 to March 5, 2008. The contract did not stipulate a specific work position or responsibility for the Defendant. During the performance period of the contract, the Plaintiff company did not restrict the work of the Defendant. Although he was occupied with welding and its improvement work, that was not the whole of his work. He also joined in other projects in the Research and Development Center including improvements to the folding door hinge of horizontal refrigerators. It can be recognized that all work completed by the Defendant in the Plaintiff company were tasks assigned to him by Wuhan Haier

Refrigerator Ltd. When the Defendant handed over his work before leaving the company, he submitted a handover list, which definitely included the technology proposal which is the subject of this case. So, we can make a judgment that the relevant technology proposal is the result of completed project work of the Defendant. The Defendant, as an employee of the Plaintiff, worked in the Quality Improvement and R&D Center. The duties of the Center are to improve defective products manufactured and sold by the company. As a professional, the Defendant signed a labor agreement with the Plaintiff, and the company's reason for employing him was for the provision of technology assistance. The improvement proposal and drawings provided by the Defendant were completed during his period of working in the Quality Improvement and R&D Center; the proposal cannot be separated from the working environment of the Center. Later demonstrations and simulation experiments were completed by Wuhan Haier Refrigerator Ltd. In discussions and the signed Patent Application Transfer Agreement between the two parties, it was stipulated that the patent was the outcome of an on-duty invention, and the Plaintiff has the rights to the patent application. Whether oral or written, the agreement was effective and the patent can be recognized as an on-duty invention.

CASE NO. 10

Shanghai Hongqi Yonghe Food Development Stock Ltd Vs. Qiao Hongxia
2009
Intermediate People's Court of Hengshui City Hebei Province

TRADEMARK INFRINGEMENT

The Plaintiff owns exclusive approved rights to use the relevant trademarks in mainland China. Without permission from the Plaintiff, the Defendant used the "Young He" images, pictures of a head capped with a straw hat and a child capped with straw hat, on his signboard and cabinets. The pictures are definitely the same as the Plaintiff's four registered trademarks.

HELD: According to the Law, the Plaintiff owns approved exclusive rights for the relevant four trademarks. The Defendant uses the relevant four trademarks illegally without permission from the Plaintiff. This action constitutes an infringement, and the defendant should cease the infringement immediately.

CASE NO. 11

Jinan Wode Automobile Parts Ltd Vs. Shanghai Xuntai Industry and Trade Ltd.
2009
People's Court of Pudong New District, Shanghai City

TRADEMARK EXCLUSIVE RIGHTS DISPUTE

The Plaintiff is the owner of "Shanhe" trademarks. Its manufactured engine valves are specific components for Heavy Automobile, First Automobile, Dongfeng Automobile and tens of other automobile plants. The Defendant sold fake products with the "Shanhe" trademark at its place of business.

HELD: Exclusive rights to the registered trademarks for an enterprise's legal entity are protected by Law. Without permission from the party which registered the trademarks, others cannot use the same or similar trademarks on the same or similar goods. Vendors who sell trademark infringed goods are violating exclusive rights to registered trademarks. Regarding determination of the amount of compensation, neither party can provide evidence for losses and benefits arising from the infringement. Therefore, reasonable compensation should be determined according to the types of goods, the status of sales and the benefits to the Defendant, and the usage rate of intake and exhaust valves manufactured by the Plaintiff.

CASE NO. 12

Beijing Quanjing Shituo Pictures Ltd Vs. Fuzhou Daily News and Tianjin Zhongxin Pharmaceutical Group Corporation Limited.
2008
Intermediate People's Court of Fuzhou City

BUSINESS PROPERTY RIGHTS

Fuzhou Evening Newspaper is sponsored by *Fuzhou Daily News*. The Defendant Darentang Pharmaceutical Factory is a branch of Tianjin Zhongxin Pharmaceutical Group Corporation Limited. An advertisement was published in *Fuzhou Evening Newspaper* for Darentang Pharmaceutical Factory for "China Time-honored Brand Tianjin Darentang" in which a photograph was used to which the Plaintiff owns copyright.

HELD: The image in the Defendant's advertisement was a simple reproduction of a photograph to which the Plaintiff owns copyright. The Defendant Darentang Pharmaceutical Factory used the relevant photograph without getting permission from the Plaintiff; in other words, the action, without any payment to the Plaintiff, constitutes a copyright infringement. Darentang Pharmaceutical Factory being a branch of an enterprise, has no independent competence to bear responsibility, so the consequences of the infringement should be borne by its head office, Tianjin Zhongxin Pharmaceutical Group Corporation Limited. The first Defendant *Fuzhou Daily News*, being a press agency for magazines, should check the contents of any publication on its press to confirm it has not violated the legal entitlements of others. However, *Fuzhou Daily News* did not make checks, leading to publication of the infringing picture in the *Fuzhou Evening Newspaper*. *Fuzhou Evening Newspaper* is sponsored by *Fuzhou Daily News*, which should bear the civil responsibility for the infringement,

CASE NO. 13

Guangdong Suihong Culture Development Ltd Vs. Chongqing High Tech District New Green Net Bar Yuying
2009
Fifth Intermediate People's Court of Chongqing

BUSINESS PROPERTY INFRINGEMENT DISPUTE
The Plaintiff owns the exclusive network distribution rights for *Contract Lover* in mainland China. The Defendant played the movie *Contract Lover* on its local area network without getting permission from or paying fees to the Plaintiff.

HELD: The Defendant placed the movie *Contract Lover* with the server of its local area network, enabling user to view the movie through the local area network. The Defendant's actions were to disseminate the movie through the Internet. However, the Plaintiff owns exclusive network dissemination rights for the movie and its protection by Law should be inviolate. At the beginning and the end of the movie, Siyuan Company is identified as the producer. The Defendant should know that the rights for network dissemination of the movie can be authorized only by the copyright owner. However, the Defendant played the movie *Contract Lover* over its local area network without getting permission from the Plaintiff and, viewed objectively, the action was a deliberate offence. The Defendant's playing of *Contract Lover* to the public by network dissemination violates the network dissemination rights of the Plaintiff. Chongqing High Tech District New Green Net Bar Yuying should bear responsibility for the infringement.

CASE NO. 14

Beijing Tianyu Tongsheng Information Technology Ltd Vs. Chongqing Yubei Green Boat Karaoke
2009
First Intermediate People's Court of Chongqing

COPYRIGHT INFRINGEMENT DISPUTE
Through authorization, the Plaintiff acquired the exclusive operating rights for *Lover Not Too Many* MTV music & player work. The Defendant played the relevant work at its place of business, without getting permission from the Plaintiff.

HELD: Authorized by the original copyright owner HIM International, the Plaintiff acquired legally exclusive Karaoke rights to the work for mainland China, and has the right to prosecute any third party who infringes the copyright. The Defendant played the relevant work at its place of business, without getting permission from the Plaintiff. The action infringed the relevant copyright owned by the Plaintiff. The Defendant should bear civil responsibility for ceasing the infringement and paying compensation for losses. Regarding the amount of compensation, the nature and art level of the work, the scale of the Defendant's operations, the duration of the Defendant's use the work and the status of the possible benefits gained should be given comprehensive consideration.

CASE NO. 15

Beijing Rongxinda Films & TV Ltd Vs. China Telecom Stock Ltd, China Telecom Stock Ltd Hubei Branch
2009
Intermediate People's Court of Hengshui City Hebei Province

RIGHTS TO NETWORK DISSEMINATION OF INFORMATION
The Plaintiff acquired the rights to network dissemination of information for the movie *Baober in Love*. The Defendant China Telecom Stock Ltd Hubei Branch displayed the movie *Baober in Love* on its website.

HELD: The Defendant was playing the relevant movie on its own website without the permission of the copyright owner. Therefore, the action of the Defendant China Telecom Stock Ltd, Hubei Brach in playing the movie on its controlled website infringed the Plaintiff's right to network dissemination of information and the Defendant should bear responsibility for infringement. The Defendant is a branch of China Telecom Stock Ltd and, although the Defendant is not qualified as a separate legal person, it can still appear in the prosecution on its own behalf. The Defendant China Telecom Stock Ltd, Hubei Branch committed the controlled infringement, in which China Telecom Stock Ltd had no involvement. According to the records of China Telecom Stock Ltd, its branches include the Hubei Branch, which should bear the rights and liabilities under the adjusted legal entity system. Furthermore, being an enterprise with the benefits of economies of scale, the Defendant can bear civil responsibility. The operating system adopted by China Telecom Stock Ltd is that civil responsibilities of branches are independent of head office; otherwise, they will have a negative effect on the operating model. Meanwhile, when the branch can bear civil responsibility, it will not cause damage to the benefits of the copyright owner. Therefore, China Telecom Stock Ltd itself need not carry civil responsibility for the infringements of China Telecom Stock Ltd, Hubei Branch.

CASE NO. 16

Center Music Company (Shenzhen) Ltd Vs. Chongqing Yubei Green Boat Music Building
2009
First Intermediate People's Court of Chongqing

WORK PROPERTY DISPUTE
The Plaintiff has the authorized exclusive rights for the *Flower in Dream (Zhang Shaohan)* MTV music & player work in mainland China. The Defendant played the relevant work to the public for profit by way of Karaoke.

HELD: Without permission from the Plaintiff, the Defendant played the relevant work for profit at its place of business. The Defendant should bear civil responsibility for ceasing the infringement and paying compensation. In calculating the amount of compensation for loss, it should comprehensively consider the nature and art level of the relevant work, the scale of the Defendant's operation, the period during which the Defendant used the related works and the profits generated.

CASE NO. 17

Center Music Company (Shenzhen) Vs. Shanghai Xianzi Entertainment Ltd
2009
People's Court of Yangpu Shanghai City

WORK PROPERTY DISPUTE

The Plaintiff has exclusive rights to the MTV work of *Fan Weiqi One to One* (Completed Version) for mainland China. Without authorization, the Defendant played the MTV work illegally to the public through the medium of Karaoke.

HELD: Through its exclusive authorization, the Plaintiff has the right to play the related MTV work in authorized Karaoke premises in mainland China, and to collect fees accordingly. Therefore, the Defendant should first get permission from the Plaintiff before playing the relevant MTV work at its place of business. The Defendant cannot provide evidence to prove they have permission from the Plaintiff to use the work, and should bear civil responsibility for ceasing to infringe and for paying compensation. The following factors should be taken comprehensively into account to determine the amount of compensation to be paid by the Defendant: the duration of the infringement by Shanghai Xianzi Entertainment Ltd, the frequency and way in which the relevant work was used, the scale of operation, operating premises located in the Zhongyuan area, Yangpu District, Shanghai, the degree of deliberate offence, the production cost and popularity of the MTV work and the economic status of the City.

CASE NO. 18

Cartier International NV Vs. Hubei Tongtian Hotel Ltd. 2009
Intermediate People's Court of Changsha City Hunan Province

TRADEMARK EXCLUSIVE RIGHTS DISPUTE

The Plaintiff is the owner of the Cartier brand. The Defendant sold fake Cartier watches at its place of business.

HELD: Selling goods that violate a registered trademark constitutes an infringement of registered trademark exclusive rights. The Plaintiff is the entity which registered the trademark and its registered trademark is protected by Law. The third party Zhangzan did not provide evidence of legal origin for his products and should bear civil responsibility accordingly. Therefore, we should support the Plaintiff's application requesting the third party to cease infringement and compensate for loss. In order to avoid consequent public confusion and to clarify the party with civil responsible, the Defendant should identify shops which are not self-operated or other sales operations in wine shop outlets, and to state that the products are not for sale in wine shop outlets.

CASE NO. 19

Honda Motor Co. Ltd Vs. Beian Century Economy Trade Ltd.
2009
People's Court of Pudong New District, Shanghai City

TRADEMARK EXCLUSIVE RIGHTS DISPUTE

The Plaintiff is the owner of the famous "HONDA" trademark. The Defendant uses the trademark on its own products without permission from the Plaintiff.

HELD: The Plaintiff owns exclusive rights to the registered trademark, and should be protected by Law. The Defendant uses the identical name "HONDA" registered trademark on its exported sparking plug without permission from the Plaintiff, which can mislead consumers on the origin of its goods. The actions of the Defendant constitute an infringement of the Plaintiff's registered trademarks and it should bear civil responsibility to cease infringement and pay compensation.

CASE NO. 20

Taishan Plasterboard Stock Ltd Vs Tu Yonghua
2009
Intermediate People's Court of Nanchang City Jiangxi Province

TRADEMARK EXCLUSIVE RIGHTS DISPUTE
The Plaintiff is the owner of the registered trademark "Taishan" for paperbacked plasterboard. The Defendant sold plasterboard with a similar trademark and design to the Plaintiff's registered "Taishan" trademark.

HELD: The Plaintiff is the owner of registered trademark "Taishan" for paperbacked plasterboard. The Defendant sold plasterboard with similar trademark and decoration to the Plaintiff's registered trademark "Taishan", leading to confusion of the paperbacked plasterboard produced by the Plaintiff, misguiding consumers to believe products of the Defendant are of the Plaintiff. The actions of the Defendant infringed the Plaintiff's exclusive right of trademark. The Defendant should stop selling the product. The Defendant has provided legal origin for the sold plasterboard. According to regulations of trademark law, the Defendant needn't to bear compensation responsibility.

CASE NO. 21

People's Court Publishing House, Beijing Wanguo Fayuan Education Technology Ltd Vs. Niu Zhenshui
2009
Intermediate People's Court of Laiwu City Shandong Province

PUBLICATION RIGHTS DISPUTE

The Plaintiff Beijing Wanguo Fayuan Education Technology Ltd is the legal publisher of *Wanguo Judicature Examination Assisting Series* books, and signed a Literature Publishing Contract with co-Plaintiff People's Publishing House, granting exclusive publishing rights for the book series. The Defendant sold pirate version of the books.

HELD: The Plaintiff Beijing Wanguo Fayuan Education Technology Ltd is the legal publisher of *State Judicature Examination Guiding* series, and transferred exclusive publishing rights to co-Plaintiff People's Publishing House. People's Publishing House owns exclusive publishing rights for the duration of the transfer. Without getting permission from People's Publishing House, the Defendant sold copies of the *State Judicature Examination Guiding* book series privately. His illegal action is prohibited by copyright laws, which damaged the exclusive publishing rights of the Plaintiff from an objective viewpoint. There is a cause and effect relationship between the two parties. From a subjective viewpoint, the Defendant, being a book distributor, has a duty to check the legal origin of goods. However, the Defendant did not verify the legal origin of those books to be sold privately. His action is an offence, and he should bear civil responsibility for compensation.

CASE NO. 22

Shanghai Yingge Import & Export Ltd Vs. Wang Xiuping 2009
People's Court of Pudong New District, Shanghai City

BUSINESS CONFIDENTIALITY DISPUTE

The Plaintiff has signed a Labor Contract with the Defendant, which stipulates that the Defendant has a duty to maintain confidentiality. The Plaintiff has undertaken a serious duty of confidentiality to manage its clients' information, quotations and other operating information. The Defendant left the company without approval from the Plaintiff and without giving notification of her departure, and she refused to hand over her current work. The Defendant then made use of the list of many clients' names and their pricing information acquired during her work to compete for the clients of the Plaintiff.

HELD: In the first instance, the Plaintiff assigned a salesman to attend the Canton Fair to acquire information about clients, and identify closely the needs of clients through further communication and business contact, including transaction habits, price, content and so on, which differentiates its enterprise list from publicly available methods. Secondly, the acquired business information has practical application; the information illustrates the needs of clients and is an important resource for the Plaintiff to pursue opportunities to do business, which can also bring economic benefits to the Plaintiff. Credit vouchers provided by the Plaintiff proves that the Plaintiff was doing business with two clients for quite a short time, but that transactions were relatively stable transactions during that period. Finally, the Plaintiff adopted confidentiality measures for the protection of operating information. The Labor Contract between the two parties and the Employee Handbook, stipulate that the Defendant must keep confidential business information, clients' information, factory information and sales and purchasing information, both during employment and after leaving. The Defendant must not use the client resources of the company and the Plaintiff paid a confidentiality fee to the Defendant. In this way the Plaintiff took certain confidentiality measures to protect its clients' information. Therefore, the Defendant bears a duty to keep the two clients' information confidential. The Defendant's business e-mail account was set by the Defendant in the name of the Defendant with passwords, which are controlled and used by the Defendant. It is illegal for the Plaintiff to get evidence from the Defendant's e-mail and such evidence is inadmissible. Meantime, e-mails provided by the Plaintiff to prove transactions between the Defendant and the clients are dated after the Defendant left the company. Although the Plaintiff can enter the e-mails, the Plaintiff should provide related evidences to verify those emails that it provided and prove that there were transactions between the Defendant and clients. However, the Plaintiff is unable to provide such evidence. Therefore, the Plaintiff's existing evidence cannot prove that the Defendant has violated business confidentiality, and the Plaintiff should bear responsibility for its inability to provide evidence.

CASE NO. 23

Yuan Kai Yin Vs. Liu Yunhua
2009
Intermediate People's Court of Changsha City Hunan Province

EXTERIOR DESIGN PATENT DISPUTE

The Plaintiff legally owns the exterior design patent for a hair washing bed (YB-9168). The Defendant sold the same hair washing bed in its own Xinyun Cosmetics & Grooming Goods Shop in Hunan Gaoqiao Market Yuhua District Shanghai City.

HELD: The Plaintiff is the owner of the exterior design patent for a hair washing bed and its legal ownership should be protected by Law. Hair washing beds sold by the Defendant are the same as the Plaintiff's, with patent No. ZL 2007 3 0304572X for a hair washing bed (YB-9168). The two kinds of products are similar in exterior design. The action of the Defendant violated the exterior design patent of the Plaintiff and the Defendant should bear civil responsibility for ceasing to infringe and for paying compensation for loss. In assessing the amount of compensation, comprehensive consideration should be given to the typof the patent, nature of the infringement, its extent and reasonable fees paid by the Plaintiff to stop the infringement.

CASE NO. 24

Hu Wuyi Vs Yeyun and Yongkang City Building Tool Company
2009
Intermediate People's Court of Changsha City Hunan Province

INVENTION PATENT RIGHTS DISPUTE

The Plaintiff owns the invention patent right for "one kind of welding plier conductor". The Defendant sells or manufactures "Lao de 300", a welding plier of which all the technology features are the same as those of the Plaintiff's patented product.

HELD: The Plaintiff Hu Wuyi is the legal owner of Patent No. ZL91104618.6, which should be protected by Law. The second Defendant Yongkang City Building Tool Company manufactures products that are the same as the Plaintiff's patented product, without getting permission from the Plaintiff, which constitutes a violation of the Plaintiff's patent. The actions of the first Defendant Yeyun who sold the infringing products, also constitute violation of the Plaintiff's patent. Regarding the amount of compensation for the infringement, the status of losses to the Plaintiff and benefits to the Defendant is unclear. The Plaintiff's claims are based on its patent implementation approval fees, allowing a reasonable time to determine further compensation.

CASE NO. 25

Kong Lingsuo Vs. Shanghai Jindun Fire Controlling Safety Equipment Ltd
2009
Higher People's Court of Shanghai

PATENT APPLICATION RIGHTS DISPUTE

The Plaintiff is a technician for the Defendant. Within the Defendant company's organization, the Plaintiff is a person in charge of researching a "Foam Spraying Fire Extinguishing System for Tunnels". The Defendant company applied to the State Intellectual Property Authority for a patent for the application of a new type of system. The Plaintiff did not agree, and therefore filed a court prosecution.

HELD: Firstly, according to the "Interface Information Dealing Tracing list" and "Work Conclusion and Planning" departments, the two parties agree in statements taken from them that the Plaintiff, being a technician of the Defendant, accepted an assignment to research a high speed water foam head for the Foam Spraying Fire Extinguishing System For Tunnels. Therefore, the Combined High Speed Water Foam Head technology was completed by the Plaintiff after receiving the Defendant's assignment. Secondly, the Defendant organized the relevant department to research the high speed water foam head for the Foam Spraying Fire Extinguishing System For Tunnels program, and undertook trials for manufacturing the product. Therefore, the Plaintiff has used the technology of the Defendant. Because the relevant technology was completed as an assignment of the Plaintiff, who also used the Defendant's existing technology, the new technology should be classified as an on-duty invention. The patent application rights should belong to the Defendant company.

CASE NO. 26

Liu Wangyang Vs. Chongqing Times Agency
2009
First Intermediate People's Court of Chongqing

COPYRIGHT INFRINGEMENT DISPUTE
The Plaintiff owns the copyright for *Crane Dancing Cloud Flying*. The Defendant used the work without the Plaintiff's consent and then revised the work, again without the written authorization of the Plaintiff or paying fees to the Plaintiff.

HELD: The relevant work is an art form for recording the profiles of selected products on sensitized material for other Media with the help of devices, in effect a photographic work. The Plaintiff owns the picture and the original negative, and the Defendant can provide no evidences to prove that others own the copyright for the work, or evidence that it was created as on-duty work assigned by others. Therefore, the Plaintiff is recognized as the owner of the work. The Defendant also approved use of the picture which it placed in an advertisement published in the *Chongqing Times* on November 5, 2008 that is identical to the work in question. Through comparison, the picture in the advertisement was copied from the work of which the Plaintiff owns the copyright. The Defendant should bear responsibility for infringement compensation for use of the work in the *Chongqing Times* on November 5, 2008.

CASE NO. 27

Shanghai Naikai Electrics Ltd Vs. Shanghai Yuanbei Information Technology Ltd, Shanghai Yuanli Numerical Control Machines Ltd and Shanghai Zhongtang Electrics Technology Ltd
2009
First Intermediate People's Court of Shanghai

COMPUTER SOFTWARE COPYRIGHT DISPUTE
The Plaintiff owns the copyright for the numerical control system, Ncstudio software. Without getting permission from the Plaintiff, the third Defendant, Shanghai Zhongtang Electrics Technology Ltd, copied the Plaintiff's Ncstudio software on disc, which it then provided to the second Defendant, Shanghai Yuanli Numerical Control Machines Ltd. The second Defendant then provided the copied software and its "Yuanli" computer carving machine to the first Defendant, Shanghai Yuanbei Information Technology Ltd. for sale to final users. The second Defendant provides a public downloading service for Ncstudio software.

HELD: The second and third Defendants jointly copied and sold the relevant software discs, for which the Plaintiff owns the software copyright. These Defendants' actions violated the copyright and publishing rights owned by the Plaintiff, and should jointly bear civil responsibility for ceasing the infringement and paying compensation. The first Defendant, Shanghai Yuanbei Information Technology Ltd, signed a Sales Contract with a person unrelated to the case, which can be mutually proved by reference to discs II. Therefore, it can be recognized that the discs II sold by the first Defendant were acquired from the third Defendant, Shanghai Zhongtang Electrics Technology Ltd. As a vendor of the relevant copied products, the first Defendant can provide the legal origin for those copied products and need not bear legal responsibility on this count. However, the first Defendant did not provide relevant evidence proving legal origin for Weihong 5.449

software granted to customers when selling control cards. Meantime, the First Defendant's employee, Xu Haoran Xu, stated in the Guarantee Book that the software acquired from Shanghai Yuanbei Information Technology Ltd was provided by e-mails. Therefore, the software was not bought by the first Defendant for resale, but copied via e-mails. Hence, the action of the first Defendant has violated the copyright and publishing rights owned by the Plaintiff, and Shanghai Yanbai Information Technology Ltd should bear civil responsibility for ceasing infringement and paying compensation; However, this case is independent of the case against the second and third Defendants.

CASE NO. 28

Guozi Film Ltd Vs. China Telecom Stock Ltd Wuhan Branch and Wuhan Changjiang Mutual Media Ltd
2009
Intermediate People's Court of Wuhan City Hubei Province

INFRINGEMENT OF NETWORK DISSEMINATION OF INFORMATION RIGHTS DISPUTE
The Plaintiff holds the copyright of Cape No.7. The two Defendants supplied videos on demand of Cape No.7. and on the website: www.wuhan.net.cn

HELD: The Plaintiff is the original owner of Cape No.7. The controlled website Yellow Crane Cinema, operated mutually by the two Defendants, China Telecom Stock Ltd Wuhan Branch and Wuhan Changjiang Mutual Media Ltd, played the relevant movie online, without getting permission from the Plaintiff, which constitutes infringement. Therefore, the two Defendants should bear joint civil responsibility for ceasing infringement and paying mutual compensation for losses to the Plaintiff.

CASE NO. 29

Wangyu Vs. China TieTong Group Gao Linjun
2008
First Intermediate People's Court of Shanghai

WORK PROPERTY INFRINGEMENT DISPUTE
The Plaintiff owns the copyright for Xichun Drawing of *The Twelve Beauties of Jinling*. The Defendant, the Hunan branch of China TieTong Group Gao Linjun, used illegally the Xichun Drawing of *The Twelve Beauties of Jinling*, originated by the Plaintiff, on its published telephone cards to promote sales.

HELD: The Defendant used the Xichun Drawing originated by the prosecutor illegally on its published telephone cards. Therefore, the action of Hunan branch of China TieTong Group Gao Linjun has violated the copyright, publishing and licensing rights owned by the Prosecutor. Furthermore, the Defendant deleted the signature and stamp on the bottom left corner of the drawin, so that the Defendant has also violated the Plaintiff's recognized signature. Because Hunan branch of China TieTong Group Gao Linjuin has violated the copying, publishing and licensing rights of the Plaintiff on its published telephone cards, the Group itself should be joined in the Plaintiff's claim and should make an apology and pay compensation. Regarding the amount of compensation, because the Plaintiff is unable to provide proof of losses and the Defendant's benefits arising from the infringement, the following should be comprehensively taken into account in arriving at the amount of compensation to be paid by the Defendant: the popularity of the work, the value and effect of the art work on the infringing controlled telephone card, the Defendant's deliberate offence and the effects of the infringement.

CASE NO. 30

Chongqing Zongshen Technology Development Ltd Vs. Chongqing Yongsheng Die-casting Ltd
2009
First Intermediate People's Court of Chongqing

PATENT RIGHTS DISPUTE

The Plaintiff is the patent owner of the outer designs for a motor wheel with patent No. ZL02302793.2. The Defendant produced and sold the relevant wheel without permission from the Plaintiff.

HELD: Without getting permission from the patent owner, the Defendant produced and sold products that violated the outer design of the Plaintiff's product patent. The Defendant should bear civil responsibility for ceasing violation and paying compensation. Because the Plaintiff did not provide evidence of loss and the benefits for the Defendant arising from the infringement, the degree of innovation in the patent, the selling price of the infringing product, the duration and range of the infringement, and reasonable fees paid by the Plaintiff for investigation and stopping the infringement should be taken comprehensively into account in determining the amount of compensation payable.

CASE NO. 31

Lu Futong Vs. Shenzhen Hengfa Daily Texture Ltd and WalMart Eastern Ltd
2008
First Intermediate People's Court of Shanghai

PATENT RIGHTS DISPUTE

The Plaintiff is the patent owner for a new and practical "no bottomless & self-opening mosquito net". The first Defendant, Shenzhen Hengfa Daily Texture Limited, produced a "Menglida Mongolia Leisure mosquito net", which was sold in supermarkets including WalMart. Upon comparison, the products manufactured and sold by the two Defendants respectively include all the technology features of the Plaintiff's patented product.

HELD: The infringing products use elastic bracing to support a complete net, consisting of a net covering on the top. Therefore, the infringing products include the technology features of a "complete net including front, rear, left and right sides and top and bottom net sheets". The products are the same as the Plaintiff's patented product in respect of other essential technology features and include all their technology features. The identified infringement is within the scope of protection for the Plaintiff's patented product. The Defendant, Shenzhen Hengfa Daily Texture Ltd, manufactured the infringing products without the patent owner's permission. Thus Hengfa Company's actions have infringed the Plaintiff's patent rights. Evidence provided by the second Defendant, WalMart Eastern Ltd, proves that the products they sell have legal origin. The Plaintiff also has no evidence to prove that WalMart Eastern Ltd knew that the first Defendant manufactured and sold the products without permission from the patent owner. Therefore, the second Defendant, Wal-Mart Eastern Ltd, need not bear responsibility for compensation, but should stop selling the infringing products.

CASE NO. 32

Zhangzhe Supor Stock Ltd Vs. Liang Qiaomei and Zhou Chunqiu
2009
Intermediate People's Court of Pingxiang City Jiangxi Province

EXCLUSIVE TRADEMARK RIGHTS AND UNFAIR COMPETITION DISPUTE

The Plaintiff is the trademark owner of "Supor". The first Defendant, Liang Qiaomei, used the Praintiff's trademark "Supor" on its own products without permission from the Plaintiff. The second Defendant, Zhou Chunqiu, sold the infringing products.

HELD: Lianjiang City Jiafu Electrics Company uses similar package and decoration with the famous trademark "Supor" on the outer packaging of its own products, additionally with the words "controlled by Supor Electrics Stock Ltd", thereby misleading consumers to believe that the Defendant's product has some relationship with the Plaintiff's product. The Defendant made use of the prosecutor's marketing strengths to promote its own products, which constitutes unfair competition to the Plaintiff. The Defendant should bear civil responsibility for ceasing the infringement and paying compensation. As proprietor of Lianjiang City Jiafu Electrics Company, Liang Qiaomei is also a proper Defendant. Therefore, the Court should support the Plaintiff's demand for Liang Qiaomei to cease the unfair competition action. The Defendant Zhou Chunqiu cannot provide evidence to prove a legal origin for those products sold, and accordingly should bear the cost of compensation. The Plaintiff's application to destroy the infringing products has no factual basis – as the Plaintiff cannot provide evidence that the Defendants have stocks of the infringing products, the application cannot be supported.

CASE NO. 33

Shanghai Shikumen Brewing Ltd Vs. Shaoxing Yuegong Brewing Company, Shanghai Tinglian Ltd and Jieqiangyingxiang Supermarket of Shanghai Wangrong Industrial and Trade Ltd
2009
First Intermediate People's Court of Shanghai

OUTER DESIGN PATENT DISPUTE

The Plaintiff is the outer design patent owner of "Shikumen" Shanghai aged wine. The first Defendant, Shaoxing Yuegong Brewing Company, produces "Tinglian" Shanghai ageing wine, of which the label has a similar outer design to that of the Plaintiff. The second Defendant, Shanghai Tinglian Ltd, produces and sells "tinglian" Shanghai ageing wine. The third Defendant Jieqiangyingxiang Supermarket of Shanghai Wangrong Industrial and Trade Ltd sells "tinglian" Shanghai ageing wine produced by the first Defendant, Shaoxing Yuegong Wine Company.

HELD: The Plaintiff legally owns the outer design patent right to the label "Shanghai Ageing Wine 2001". Without permission from the Plaintiff, no-one is allowed to produce, sell and import products subject to that outer design patent for their production operations. The main features of the Plaintiff's patented labels are shape, the colour combination of gold and burgundy, the Shikumen pattern and the arrangement of numbers and characters. Comparing the infringing labels with those of the Plaintiff, the two shapes are the same, the backgrounds are all in gold, and use burgundy to sketch similar outlines of Shikumen. Shikumen images are also integrated in the door header, door plate and doorpost, and are presented in the same way with the same shape and color combination. Although there are differences in the flowers included in the door header, the numbers on the door plate and characters on the door, viewing the two labels from an overall perspective, they are similar and would be easily confused by ordinary consumers. Therefore, the infringing label in question should be considered to be within scope of protection for the Plaintiff's patented labels. The first Defendant, Shaoxing Yuegong Wine Company, produced and sold yellow rice or millet wine with the infringing labels, without getting permission from the Plaintiff, which has violated the Plaintiff's patented outer design for the label "Shanghai Aging Wine 2001". The Defendant should bear civil responsibility to cease the infringement and pay compensation. The relevant yellow rice or millet wine labels bear the trademark of the second Defendant, Shanghai Tinglian Ltd, and its function is to identify the origin of goods and to guide consumers to recognize that the relevant yellow rice or millet wine is a product of Shanghai Tinglian Ltd, or has some relationship to the company. The second Defendant is clear about the manner of its labeling and the effect. The second and first Defendants have a joint arrangement to produce and sell the relevant yellow rice or millet wine, with an agreed division of labor. In practice, the first Defendant, Shaoxing Yuegong Brewery Company, is responsible for production, while the second Defendant, Shanghai Tinglian Ltd, is responsible for sales and marketing of the infringing product. Therefore, the actions of the two Defendants constitute mutual infringement and they should mutually bear civil responsibility to cease the infringement and pay compensation. The third Defendant, Jieqiangyinxiang Supermarket of Shanghai Wangrong Industrial Trade Ltd, sold the relevant yellow rice or millet wine, for which it cannot confirm the legal origin. According to Chapter 63, item 2 of the Patent Law of the People's Republic of China, the third Defendant should not only bear civil responsibility for ceasing its infringement, but also make compensation.

CASE NO. 34

Shanghai Lingke Technology Ltd Vs. Shanghai Juxin Automatic Technology Ltd
2008
First Intermediate People's Court of Shanghai

BUSINESS PROPERTY RIGHTS DISPUTE

The Defendant uses the images on its website for which the Plaintiff owns the copyright.

HELD: For business purpooses, the Plaintiff commissioned Churen Company, not a party to the case, to print a promotional booklet. The relevant seven pictures were of the Plaintiff's product design and real life examples of installations, which were provided by the Plaintiff to Churen Company. Without evidence to the contrary, it can be acknowledged that the Plaintiff owns copyright for the relevant seven pictures. The Defendant uploaded images of the relevant seven pictures onto its website for its use, without getting permission from the Plaintiff; the action constitutes infringement of the Plaintiff's copyright. Accordingly, the Defendant should bear civil responsibility. In determining the amount of compensation due, because the Plaintiff did not provide evidence of loss and the Defendant's benefits resulting from the infringement, the type of the works, the manner, duration and range of influence of the infringement, the Defendant's deliberate offence and reasonable fees paid by the Plaintiff for bringing the case to Court should be taken comprehensively into consideration.

CASE NO. 35

WLNET(Beijing) Technology Vs. Shanghai Gaoqin Communication Technology Ltd.
2009
People's Court of Pudong New District Shanghai City

BUSINESS PROPERTY RIGHTS DISPUTE
The Plaintiff owns exclusive rights to internet dissemination of content for the reception of movies by computer in mainland China. Without getting permission, the Defendant provided links to the relevant movie on its website.

HELD: The Plaintiff owns the legal right to internet dissemination of content for the relevant movie. Anyone who provides the relevant movie playing service by internet dissemination, without permission or beyond reasonable use under exempted responsibility, violates the Plaintiff's right to internet dissemination of content. In this case, the person who directly uploaded the movie *Brothers* to "mofang" website is a registered user of the website. The Defendant provided storage space on its website for the user. Under the editing arrangements of the Defendant's website, contents are divided into original, entertainment, music, movie, plays and others. The arrangements are not only convenient for users to upload content, but also for the public to select content for viewing. The arrangements also allow the Defendant to check the content uploaded by users, in order to avoid illegal actions or infringements. On the other hand, the arrangements also offer a convenient way to disseminate infringing products on the internet. The production of films and TV programs takes substantial human and financial resources. Usually, the owners of films and TV programs will not provide free downloading or playing services to the public on the internet. Therefore, the Defendant who specializes in videos for movies and TV programs and other entertainment, should take superior responsibility for checking movies and TV programs uploaded on its website, especially for those that are popular. After cataloguing

Brothers, there are many videos of the movie in existence uploaded by different users at different times. The Defendant should acknowledge copyright for each such case as a daily routine. However, the Defendant ignored its duty and allowed the infringement to continue. As a video sharing website, the Defendant provided net space; although the Defendant did not itself implement the uploading service directly, the Defendant helped users to upload the infringing video. The Defendant has committed a deliberate offence and should bear civil responsibility to cease the infringement and pay compensation.

CASE NO. 36

Ningbo Success Media Communication Ltd Vs. Shanghai VC Network Technology Ltd
2009
People's Court of Pudong New District, Shanghai City

BUSINESS PROPERTY RIGHTS DISPUTE
The Plaintiff owns exclusive rights to internet dissemination of content for *Fit Lover*. The Defendant provided its downloading service to its users on its website without permission from the Plaintiff.

HELD: The Plaintiff owns exclusive rights to internet dissemination of content for *Fit Lover*. As an internet service provider, the Defendant provides its users with registration, "emule" software for log-in, for downloading and indexing and for operating various websites. "emule", being P2P software, allows a user to exchange data with others by linking its computer to others. From this aspect, users, rather than the website, are actually the ones to violate the Plaintiff's rights to internet dissemination of content. The purpose of the website is to provide users with "emule" software and to download content listed on the website resource. On the other hand, the Defendant revises its indexing catalog, to highlight "recommendations" and "hot resources" on its homepage. The relevant movie was listed as No.1 in both "recommendations" and "hot resources", thereby facilitating the upload and download by users of the relevant movie. There is no evidence to prove that the users who disseminated the movie were authorized by the copyright owner, so that the action of downloading the relevant movie has violated the Plaintiff's rights to internet dissemination of content. The Defendant helped users to disseminate the infringing work, which also violated the Plaintiff's rights, and should bear responsibility for ceasing the infringement.

CASE NO. 37

Getty Images China Vs. Chongqing Hotel Ltd
2009
People's Court of Yuzhong District Chongqing City

BUSINESS PROPERTY RIGHTS DISPUTE

The Plaintiff is authorized by Getty Images, Inc. with the right to exhibit, sell and permit others to use the relevant pictures in the People's Republic of China and also with the rights to take any necessary legal measures in the name of Getty Images China for any third party violation of its intellectual property (copyrights, including moral right) owned by Getty Images China, or the use of pictures without its authorization. The Defendant used a picture to which Getty Images China owns the rights in its promotional advertisement without authorization.

HELD: The Plaintiff has the right to prosecute actions of copyright infringement in the name of Getty Images China within the scope of its authorization. The Defendant used the relevant picture without authorization and should bear civil responsibility for ceasing the infringement, eliminating its effects, making an apology and paying compensation.

CASE NO. 38

Guangdong Panda Daily Chemical Products Co. Ltd. Vs. Wang Hande
2008
Changsha Intermediate People's Court

DISPUTE ON THE RIGHTS TO EXCLUSIVE USE OF TRADEMARK

The Plaintiff is the registered holder of trademark rights to "LaFanG and its figure", and the Defendant is infringing the exclusive trademark rights of "LanFanG and its figure" in respect of shampoo, hair conditioner and soap products.

HELD: The Plaintiff is the registered trademark rights holder of "LaFanG and its figure", and the exclusive use of its trademark is protected by Law. The Defendant has infringed the exclusive rights to the use of the trademark "LanFanG and its figure", which constitutes a trademark infringement. Due to the fact that the Defendant can neither prove that the infringing goods that he sold were legally obtained, nor can tell the Court who is the supplier, the Plaintiff's lawsuit requiring the Defendant to compensate the economic loss is legally based and upheld. Moreover, since the Plaintiff has failed to prove the Defendant's benefits and the losses due to the infringement, the case is subject to the applicable conditions for calculating compensation. The amount of the compensation should be determined by considering comprehensively the nature, duration and consequences of the infringement and public awareness of the trademark, as well as the reasonable expenses for stopping the infringement.

CASE NO. 39

Beijing Three-Oriented Copyright Agency Ltd. Vs. Pingxiang City Campus of Jiangxi Radio and Television University
2009
Pingxiang Intermediate People's Court, Jiangxi province

COPYRIGHT INFRINGEMENT DISPUTE
The Plaintiff acquired the copyright of *An Ecstasy Order* and other works through a transfer of rights; the Defendant, without getting authorization, has put *An Ecstasy Order* on the internet enabling it to be downloaded and distributed at random by the public.

HELD: Except for copyrights such as the right of authorship and Film and TV Adaptation Rights, the Plaintiff has acquired all the rights of *An Ecstasy Order* and is protected by Law. The Defendant put *An Ecstasy Order* on its web page and there are not any words that show that the work concerned is made available by links from another website; furthermore, the Defendant also fails to provide appropriate evidence to substantiate its claim; even if the work on the Defendant's web page is linked to another website, the Defendant still commits an infringement of the Plaintiff's copyright. Therefore, the assertion of the Defendant, that it only provides a link service and should not bear a civil infringement liability, cannot be established. The Defendant provides the work in question, *An Ecstasy Order,* to non-specific internet users on its website without any encryption, which allows network users to decide the time and place according to their preferences to receive the work involved. The Defendant's claims that its website in only for the use of school teachers and students to learn and study have no factual basis; therefore, their claims cannot be established and the Defendant's use of the copyright to *An Ecstasy Order* to which the Plaintiff is entitled does not qualify as reasonable use. The Defendant publicizes *An Ecstasy Order* to which the Plaintiff owns the copyright on its website without obtaining the Plaintiff's permission, and also fails to pay any compensation to the Plaintiff. Therefore, its behavior infringes the internet communication rights to content, and the Defendant should carry the liability of ceasing to infringe and of compensating the Plaintiff for losses.

CASE N0. 40

Wang Peng Vs. Shanghai Han Ni Di Restaurant Management Co, Ltd.
2008
New Pudong District Intermediate People's Court, Shanghai

DISPUTE ON THE RIGHTS TO EXCLUSIVE USE OF TRADEMARK

The Plaintiff is the exclusive rights holder to "Xu Liushan", and the Defendant sells the same and similar products as the Plaintiff has registered in its five dessert sales stores without receiving the Plaintiff's permission.

HELD: The Plaintiff applied for registration of the trademark in November, 2004, which was checked and approved in March, 2007, later than the Defendant's use the trademark. During the checking period, the Defendant used the trademark "Xu Liushan", which does not constitute an infringement of the exclusive rights of the Plaintiff's registered trademark.

CASE NO. 41

Guangzhou Daming United Rubber Products Co. Ltd. Vs. Chongqing Jiu-Kang Medical Instrument Co. Ltd.
2009
The 5th Chongqing Intermediate People's Court

DISPUTE ON THE RIGHTS TO EXCLUSIVE USE OF TRADEMARK

The Plaintiff is holder of the registered trademark rights of No. 1138964 "Ausny", and the Defendant is misleading consumers by selling "JIEAONI" rubber condoms.

HELD: As the transferee of the registered trademark "Ausny", the Defendant is entitled to the trademark in accordance with the Law. When comparing the combination trademark "JIEAONI" and the registered trademark "Ausny", both trademarks are composed of phonetic alphabet or English letters with similar pronunciation, and the outstanding common points of both trademarks are "AONI". Therefore, we can identify that the trademarks are similar. The registration application for the combination trademark of "JIEAONI" has been received by the State Trademark Bureau, but is not yet registered. It is verified that the usage scope of the registered trademark "Ausny" includes the condom and the combination trademark "JIEAONI" can also be applied to condoms. The action of using the combination trademark "JIEAONI", a similar trademark for the same kind of goods, constitutes an infringement of the exclusive trademark usage rights of the Plaintiff.

CASE NO. 42

Beijing Kinmen and Matsu Culture Communication Co. Ltd. Vs. Wuhan Le Di Bear Music Entertainment Co. Ltd.
2009
Wuhan Intermediate People's Court, Hubei province

COPYRIGHT DISPUTE

The Plaintiff owns the copyright of the MTV that is the subject of this case. The Defendant reproduces this MTV through an on-demand system in the "Hao Le Di" KTV private rooms and show it to the public without authorization in the form of Kara for the purpose of gaining profits without authorization.

HELD: The Plaintiff is the copyright holder of the seven items of the MTV, such as *The Wolf Falls In Love With The Sheep* and so on; its performance rights are therefore protected by Law. Without the Plaintiff's consent, the Defendant plays the seven MTV works such as *The Wolf Falls In Love With The Sheep*, thereby infringing the performance rights of the plaintiff, and should bear the liability for ceasing infringement and compensating for losses.

CASE NO. 43

Shanghai High Mountains and Long River Garments Co. Ltd. Vs. Yan Dalun and Feng Dawei
2008
Shanghai Intermediate People's Court

DISPUTE ON PROPERTY RIGHTS IN WORK
The Plaintiff owns the copyright to the Ruyi wave design. The Defendants Yan Dalun and Feng Dawei copied the design of the Plaintiff and sell dresses in the Ruyi wave design in the clothing store that they operate, without the Plaintiff's consent.

HELD: The legal representative of the Ruyi wave design is Xu Yulin, and a picture of the Ruyi wave design that is applied to clothes was published publicly in a Japanese magazine in July, 2004. Thereafter, the Plaintiff registered the copyright for a revised Ruyi wave design. Therefore, the Plaintiff owns the copyright to the Ruyi wave design, which shall be protected by Law. The Defendants use a design similar to the Ruyi wave design published in the Japanese magazine in 2004 on their own dresses, which constitutes an infringement of the Plaintiff's copyright; therefore, they should bear civil liability for compensation of losses. The first Defendant, Yan Dalun, not only provides the place of business, but also licences his individual registered industrial and commercial households letterhead to the second Defendant, Feng Dawei. The sales invoices issued by Feng Dawei also shows that Guangda clothing store in Luwan District of Shanghai that is owned by Yan Dalun is the vendor of dresses with the Ruyi wave design; both the Defendants' actions are equally damaging. The first Defendant, Yan Dalun, stipulates that the second Defendant, Feng Dawei, is the main party to bear the liability for illegal operation in their operating agreement; however, this commitment cannot override the claim of infringement on the copyright. so the Defendant Yan Dalun should bear joint civil liability.

CASE NO. 44

Aerfenna Electrical Systems Inc. Vs Zhejiang Lido Electric Co. Ltd
2007
Wenzhou Intermediate People's Court, Zhejiang Province

INFRINGEMENT DISPUTE ON FASCIA DESIGN PATENT
The Plaintiff owns the fascia design patent of "Power outlets (wiring Accessories)". The Defendant, without the permission or consent of the Plaintiff, manufactures and sells the same products as the patent protected products for commercial purposes.

HELD: The Plaintiff, Aerfenna Electrical Systems Inc. is patent holder of the fascia design of "Power outlets (Wiring Accessories)", which shall be protected by Law. The E132-B product manufactured and sold by the Defendant is identical to the patented ZL20053001464.6 fascia design product in respect if the fascia design element and overall layout of the front. There are only slight differences of detail in the position and shape of the light switch. After viewing the main picture of the patent, people who observe the E13-B product, aside from comparing them together, would consider that there is very little difference between the two products. Generally speaking, the design of the switch is embodied mainly in the front of the switch. Therefore, it is difficult to draw consumers' attention to the four ribs on the upper left corner at the back of the product accused of infringement; and these four ribs have little impact on the overall visual impression of the product. Moreover, the bump on the lower right corner also has little impact on the overall appearance of the product. The fascia design of the E13-B product manufactured and sold by the Defendant and that of the patented ZL200530001464.6 product of the Plaintiff are similar. The Defendant in this case manufactures and sells products that have a similar fascia design to the patented product during the life of the patent without the Plaintiff's permission. Therefore, the Defendant caused damage to the Plaintiff's copyright and should bear corresponding civil liability.

CASE NO. 45

Taiwan D-Link Electronic Equipment (Shanghai) Co. Ltd. Vs. Lai Changhua
2008
Huzhou Intermediate People's Court, Zhejiang province

DISPUTE ON EXCLUSIVE TRADEMARK RIGHTS
The Plaintiff owns exclusive rights to the trademarks "D-Link", "D-Link Electronic Equipment" and "D-Link Internet". Two switches which are counterfeit products of the Defendant were seized in B-33, the third floor of Ego Digital Plaza, Huzhou city.

HELD: The Plaintiff is owner of the trademarks "D-Link", "D-Link Electronic Equipment" and "D-Link Internet". After verification by China's State Administration for Industry, the company has the exclusive rights to the registered trademarks within the scope of the goods, which shall be protected by Law. Although the Defendant declares that the counterfeits of "D-Link" seized by the Wuxing branch of Huzhou Industry and Commerce Administration are bonded materials and that he had no idea that they were infringing products, the Defendant fails to provide evidence to confirm that the infringing products were obtained lawfully. Nor can he describe the provider; moreover, the Defendant also admitted if someone wanted to buy the products he would sell them during the period of the trial. Therefore, cause for the Plaintiff to take legal proceedings against the Defendant for infringement on its rights to use and derive profit (*usufruct*) from the trademarks is established, and the Defendant should bear the civil liability to compensate for economic loss.

CASE NO. 46

He Haiqun Vs. Municipal Library of Wenzhou
2009
Wenzhou Intermediate People's Court, Zhejiang province

DISPUTE ON PROPERTY RIGHTS IN WORK

The Plaintiff is the copyright holder of *Expert on Internet Business*. The Defendant publishes the book in question without authorization in its E-times library to allow internet users to download.

HELD: The Defendant, without the permission of the Plaintiff, provides the public with the search and download service of *Expert on Internet Business* in the manner of mirror infringements of the internet content communication rights of the book, and should therefore bear responsibility.

CASE NO. 47

Zhong Zhiwen Vs. Yueqing Tian Mei Tools Co. Ltd.
2009
Wenzhou Intermediate People's Court, Zhejiang province

DISPUTE ON PATENTED INVENTION

The Plaintiff is the patentee of hand tools. Without authorization, the Defendant used the patented invention to manufacture, sell and make offers of sale for the hand tool products JY-2059 and JY-2060.

HELD: JY-2059 and Jy-2060 hand tools, manufactured and sold by the Defendant have all the technical characteristics of No. ZL98 8 14169.8 patented invention owned by the Plaintiff and infringe the scope of protection of the patented invention. The Plaintiff owns the invention patent of No. ZL98 8 14169.8 and the Defendant manufactures, sells and offers for sale the patented product of the Plaintiff in the management of its production without the Plaintiff's permission. This behavior infringes the patent of the Plaintiff and the Defendant should bear civil liability for ceasing the infringement, paying compensation for losses, and so on.

CASE NO. 48

Yanghe Brewery Co. Ltd. Vs. Heyang Brewery Co. Ltd. and Shanghai Xinchen Trade Co. Ltd.
2009
Huangpu District Intermediate People's Court, Shanghai

DISPUTE ON EXCLUSIVE TRADEMARK RIGHTS
The Plaintiff holds the rights to the well-known trademark "Yanghe", and the first Defendant, Heyang Brewery Co. Ltd, uses the registered mark of the Plaintiff on the liquor that it produces without the Plaintiff's permission. The second Defendant, Shanghai Xinchen Trade Co. Ltd, is accused of selling a large amount of the infringing liquor produced by the first Defendant.

HELD: The Plaintiff holds the rights to the well-known trademark "Yanghe" and has the exclusive right to use the trademark in accordance with the Law. The registered trademark "Yanghe" was judged to be a well-known Chinese trademark by SAIC in 2002, and has enjoyed a high reputation and visibility among the public. As a producer of liquors in the same district as the Plaintiff, the Defendant must be very clear about the trademark "Yanghe". Without the Plaintiff's permission, the first Defendant, Heyang Brewery Co. Ltd, produces and sells "Zhenhuang" Guest liquor and Laojiao liquor; furthermore, "Yanghe", which is printed in the prominent position of a trademark and shares the same font as the registered trademark "Yanghe" of the Plaintiff, with the obvious intention of misleading consumers. Thus, the first Defendant infringes the Plaintiff's exclusive trademark rights. As a liquor wholesaling company, the second Defendant Shanghai Xinchen Trade Co. Ltd is the dealer for "Yanghe ZhenHuang" Guest liquor and Laojiao liquor in Shanghai; therefore, the company has an obligation to check these two brands of liquor. The second Defendant fails to fulfill its obligation to check the liquor and sells the liquor that obviously infringes the registered trademark of the Plaintiff. Both of the Defendants should bear the civil liability of ceasing the infringement and compensating for the losses.

CHINESE COURT JUDGEMENTS: INTELLECTUAL PROPERTY

PART TWO: 2004 - 2007

CASE NO. 49

Xingyuan Co. Ltd and Starbucks Coffee Company Vs. Shanghai Starbucks and Shanghai Starbucks Branch
2006
Shanghai Supreme People's Court

FAKING OF REGISTERED BRAND DISPUTE
The first Defendant, Shanghai Starbucks, uses the logo of three pentagrams and the characters which are printed on the Plaintiffs' branded glasses and screens.

HELD: The first Defendant had already known the logo of Starbucks, which has a good commercial reputation, before registering the name of the enterprise. It registered "Starbucks" for the type and size of its enterprise in order to utilize the fame and influence of "STARBUCKS" for its "Starbucks" logo and to improve its market reputation and influence. Therefore, since the first Defendant, Shanghai Starbucks, had checked and approved the type and size of its registered enterprise, it had malicious intent and does not share preferential legal rights to the name of an enterprise which includes the "Starbucks" characters. As the Defendants profited from this infringement and the two Plaintiffs suffered loss from the infringement, all of which are difficult to determine, the amounts of compensation are to be determined according to Law. The two Defendants in this case committed acts of brand infringement and unreasonable competition, and a part of the action relates to competition. For the competition part, the amount of compensation for loss due to this infringement cannot be calculated. Determination of the compensating amount will take into account the nature, duration and outcome of the two Defendants' rights infringement and the reputation and prestige of the logo of the two Plaintiffs and their reasonable expenditure. The two Plaintiffs are entitled to stop all infringing activities, which are comprehensively determined.

CASE NO. 50

The Extra-budgetary Funds Administrative Bureau of Guannan County and Liangxianghe Company Vs. Tao Qin
2006
The Higher People's Court of Jiangsu Province

COUNTERFEITING REGISTERED TRADEMARKS DISPUTE
The Plaintiff takes its geographical name as the registered trademark for its products. The Defendant also uses the same geographical name in its corporate name and product names.

HELD: Within the registered trademarks of the Plaintiff, the word "Tanggou" derives from the geographical name "Tanggou Town". However, as a result of its long-term usage by the Plaintiff as a trademark for its alcoholic products, the word "Tanggou Town" no longer has the meaning of just marking their origin, but rather has become a synonym for the Plaintiff's products. As the brand "Tanggou" involved in the case has achieved high popularity, the average consumer's first impression of the word "Tanggou" marked on alcoholic products is as a trademark, rather than just a geographical name. The Defendant highlights the use of the word "Tanggou" in its product packaging and its deliberate intention is not the legitimate purpose of marking the origin or source of its products; it can neither be categorized as "legitimate use" as defined in the provision of Article 49, Trade Marks Ordinance of China, nor as "normal use" of its business name, but rather constitutes a violation of the Plaintiff's registered trademark "Tanggou". The Defendant highlights the use of the same text as the registered trademark, without authorization, as its business brand for the same type of commodity, which is sufficient to cause consumers to misunderstand, thereby violating the Plaintiff's registered trademark rights. Therefore, the Defendant shall be liable in civil law to cease the infringement and compensate for loss. However, the infringement of the Defendant only involves the prominent use of its business brand; the enterprise name itself which includes the business brand does not constitute a trademark infringement. Therefore the Plaintiff's request for a Court order for the Defendant to change its enterprise name has no legal basis and is not upheld by the Court.

CASE NO. 51

Jinan Ward Auto Parts Co. Ltd. Vs. Wei Changjun
2007
The Intermediate People's Court of Linyi City, Shandong Province

TRADEMARK INFRINGEMENT DISPUTE

The Plaintiff acquired the exclusive rights for the registered trademark "Shanhe" by assignment. "Shanhe" brand automobile engines, intake and exhaust ports produced by the Plaintiff are specific supporting components of China National Heavy Duty Truck Group, FAW, Dongfeng and other OEMs, and enjoy a level of popularity in the automotive aftermarket. The Defendant sells a large number of counterfeit products marked with the Plaintiff's trademark without its permission.

HELD: The exclusive rights of the Plaintiff's trademark are protected by Law. The Defendant sells counterfeit products marked with the Plaintiff's registered trademark from its business premises, and such an act constitutes an infringement of the exclusive registered trademark rights of the Plaintiff.

CASE NO. 52

Bonneterie Cévenole S.A.R.L. Vs. Shanghai Meizheng Co. Ltd.
2004
The Supreme People's Court

DISPUTE OVER COUNTERFEITING AND FORGING OF WELL-KNOWN PRODUCT-SPECIFIC NAMES, PACKAGING AND DECORATION
Comparing the clothing produced by the Defendant with the trademark of the Plaintiff, the overall layout, background color, the colors of petals and bars are consistent with each other and only the text differs.

HELD: Comparing the trademark of the Defendant and the decoration of the Plaintiff's shopping bags, although the trademark and text are different, the overall decorative design style is the same; according to the general view of consumers shopping, it is very easy to confuse the two bags. The Defendant and the Plaintiff are competitors in the same industry. The intention of the Defendant in committing these acts is clearly to encourage consumers to believe mistakenly that their products in their store originate from the Plaintiff, thereby achieving its purpose of confusing its own goods with the Plaintiff's well-known products. These acts violate the principle of good faith and are sufficient to cause consumer misunderstanding of the relationship between the Defendant and the Plaintiff, to disrupt the normal conditions of market competition and to damage the legal rights and interests of the Plaintiff and relevant consumers. As a result, they constitute unfair competition.

CASE NO. 53

Guoxin Tendering Co. Ltd. v. Beijing Bidcenter Network Information Technology Co. Ltd.
2005
Beijing Second Intermediate People's Court

UNFAIR COMPETITION DISPUTE

The Plaintiff is the legal owner of "China Bidding" (the corresponding domain name of the site is: chinabidding.com.cn). On November 18, 2004, the Beijing Administration for Industry and Commerce issued a direction on the domain name of "Cnbidding" of the Defendant, ruling that the corresponding domain name of the site is: cnbidding.com.cn. The Plaintiff believes that there is a clear name similarity between "Cnbidding" applied by the Defendant and its own "China Bidding", which is sufficient to cause the misunderstanding of others and to result in unfair competition.

HELD: In the domain name "China Bidding", "China" is a geographical designation; "Bidding" refers to the industry's operating mode, and "net" is the generic domain necessary to a website name. Therefore, the domain name of "China Bidding" is devoid of distinctive features and does not have significant recognition. It follows that no similarity exists between the names of the Defendant's "Cnbidding" and the Plaintiff's "China Bidding".

CASE NO. 54

Brilliance Jinbei Company v. Jin Cheng Company
2006
The Higher People's Court of Beijing Municipality

DESIGN PATENT INFRINGEMENT DISPUTE
The Plaintiff is patentee of the appearance design of "light passenger car SY6484". The front view of this appearance design patent shows: the panel at the front section moving forward clearly and with a convex hem; the forward radiator grille is a wide grille with short beams; the short beams radiating from both sides of the grille are a long-upper and short-lower. The right and top views show: supports and bevel angles of each part of the body are linked by a large "R" arc; the panels at the right and left sides and the entire body panel form a completed continuous transition curved surface; the skirting-board near the tyres is a protruding sub-panel; and the rear elevation shows that the tail lights are arranged horizontally. For the Jin Cheng Sea Lion light passenger car manufactured by the Defendant, the only material differences are the length of the short beams on both sides of the radiator grille and that the tail lights are arranged vertically.

HELD: The Plaintiff has legal entitlement to the appearance design patent of "light passenger car SY6484", and without its permission, no entity or individual should use its patent. Comparing the appearance designs of the patented product with that of the allegedly infringing product, the light passenger car manufactured and sold by the Defendant, the appearance design of this car includes the main key design points of the Defendant's appearance design patent. Although the front radiator grille and tail light designs are slightly different, they are still basically the same or similar and the model GDQ6480A light passenger car, manufactured and sold by the Defendant, embodies an infringement of the Plaintiff's appearance design patent.

CASE NO. 55

Music Copyright Society of China v. Shenzhen Konka Telecommunications Technology Co. Ltd and Beijing Tongwanbao Commercial and Trade Co. Ltd.
2004
Beijing Second Intermediate People's Court

COPYRIGHT DISPUTE

The plaintiff and Lei Lei (author of the song *Desire*) signed a Music Copyright Contract, under the terms of which Lei Lei agreed to entrust management of the public performance rights, broadcasting rights and recording and publishing rights of their musical works to the Plaintiff. The First Defendant, Shenzehn Konka Telecommunications Technology Co. Ltd, without the authorization of the Plaintiff or the copyright holder, and without paying copyright royalties to the Plaintiff or the copyright holder, designated the song *Desire* as a ring tone for incoming calls on mobile telephones produced by the Defendant and implanted the song into its IC cards.

HELD: The Plaintiff under the terms of the contract, manages the public performance rights, broadcasting rights, recording and publishing rights of the song *Desire* on behalf of the copyright holder, and has the right to sue infringers in its own name. The first Defendant, Shenzhen Konka Telecommunications Technology Co. Ltd, uses the song *Desire* as a ring tone for incoming calls on its Konka mobile telephones Model 7688 by implanting it into IC cards. Although the duration of the ring tone is as long as 50 seconds, it does not completely demonstrate all the content of the music, but users can identify absolutely that this ring tone is a part of *Desire*. According to the Copyright Law of China, sound recording producers can reproduce sound recordings by using music that has been legally recorded as sound recordings by other persons without the permission of the copyright holder, but should pay royalty fees in accordance with the relevant provisions. The Defendant does not pay royalty fees in accordance with the relevant provisions, so that its actions violate the copyright of the song *Desire* and it shall bear corresponding legal liability according to the Law.

CASE NO. 56

Hong Qingqi v. National Palace Museum and Beijing Ideal Creative Art Design Co. Ltd.
2005
Beijing Second Intermediate People's Court

COPYRIGHT DISPUTE

In May 2004, the Forbidden City issued a "Tender Notice", publicly inviting submissions for its program to design a Museum Logo. The Plaintiff mailed his own works to the National Palace Museum. As no suitable work was submitted, in May 2005 the Forbidden City decided to announce that the selection program for this Museum Logo design was cancelled. On May 23, 2005, the Forbidden City (Party A) signed a Contract of Entrustment of Creation with the Defendant, Beijing Ideal Creative Art Design Co. Ltd (Party B). According to the contract, the Defendant completed the Museum Logo design for the National Palace Museum. The logo uses the deformation font of Chinese character and the whole Museum Logo is red. The National Palace Museum approved the above Museum Logo that has been put into actual use.

HELD: The design of the Plaintiff for the selection program involved in the case is original and belongs to the category of artworks protected by the Copyright Law of China; the copyright owned by the Plaintiff on his work shall be protected by Law. However, the Museum Logo design of the Defendant was not similar to the Plaintiff's work in Law.

CASE NO. 57

**Jiang Tao v. Xidian University Press
(2005)
Beijing Second Intermediate People's Court**

COPYRIGHT DISPUTE
The book *Grasp Wubi in Two Days – No Need to Recite the Roots* prepared and completed by the Plaintiff was published in October 2002 by the China Children Publishing House; attached to the book was a CD-ROM. The main content of the book is to teach the learning and practice of the Wubi input method. The Defendant published the CD-ROM and a book *Wubi Holiday Express* with the byline "Prepared by Three Graduates Wubi Research", and the tagline on the cover includes the text "Grasp in two days – no need to recite the roots". The main content of the book is to teach the learning and practice of the Wubi input method. In comparison, the content of the Defendant's book is not the same as that of the Plaintiff's book.

HELD: *Grasp Wubi in Two Days – No Need to Recite the Roots* was chosen by the Plaintiff as the book's name to describe the purpose to be achieved by the author through its content, which is an objective and descriptive account of the topic, and it must be combined with the content of the book before it can constitute a phrase within the meaning of Copyright Law. Separately, the sentence by itself expresses an objective situation and lacks originality. Moreover, this expression is extremely limited as a description of the objective situation; therefore, it does not constitute a work and should not be protected by the Copyright Law of China.

CASE NO. 58

AgrEvo Vs. Nanjing First Pesticide Plant
2005
The Intermediate People's Court of Nanjing

TRADEMARK INFRINGEMENT DISPUTE
The Plaintiff acquired the exclusive rights to the registered trademark of the "Cotton Boll" pattern through assignment. In March 1998, the Plaintiff discovered that the Defendant used the registered trademark of the "Cotton Boll" pattern in the external packaging labels for its products without authorization; the Plaintiff subsequently filed a lawsuit against the Defendant.

HELD: The "Cotton Boll" pattern trademark is a trademark registered with the State Trademark Bureau. The Plaintiff acquired the exclusive rights to this trademark legally by assignment and such rights are protected by Chinese Law. In the event of trademark infringement, the infringed party may claim compensation in accordance with its actual loss incurred, or in accordance with the profits of the infringing party arising from the infringement (referring to all profits excluding cost and taxes). The Defendant has the right to choose between the above two options.

CASE NO. 59

Kohler Vs. Beijing Meilian Tiandi Building Material Mart Co. Ltd and Deli Company and Kenai Company
2007
The Second Intermediate People's Court of Beijing

PATENT RIGHTS DISPUTE

The Plaintiff is the legal owner of the patent rights for "the handle and valve component" design. The Defendants produced and sold, and the first Defendant, Beijing Meilian Tiandi Building Material Mart Co. Ltd, sold products basically similar to the faucet products for the design of which the Plaintiff owns the patent rights.

HELD: The exclusive rights for the design of "handle and valve component" (patent number: ZL00337789.X) granted to the Plaintiff and approved by the State Intellectual Property Office of the People's Republic of China are still within the period of validity and shall be protected by Law. Without permission from the owner of patent rights, any working unit or person shall not exploit the patent, which means that any working unit or person shall not manufacture, sell or import products with the appearance of the patented design for purposes of production and management. As provided in the relevant Laws, the extent of protection of the patented design rights shall be determined by the product incorporating the patented design as illustrated in the accompanying drawings or photographs. The products in question bought by Plaintiff, with due notarization, from the first Defendant have the same appearance as those incorporating the patented design to which the rights are owned by the Plaintiff. Therefore, the Court concluded that the products involved in the case are products that infringe the Plaintiff's relevant patent rights. The further Defendants, Deli and Kenai, are both parties to the infringement in production and sales respectively, and both Defendants have admitted that the products concerned are manufactured and sold in the name of both companies jointly. Accordingly, the Defendants Deli and Kenai shall jointly bear civil liability for production and sales of the infringing products. The first Defendant, Beijing Meilian Tiandi Building Material Mart Co. Ltd, sourced legitimately the infringing products, which it is selling. Therefore, the first Defendant shall not be held liable for compensation but shall be responsible for stopping sales.

CASE NO. 60

Danfoss Company Vs. Zibo-based Danfosi Detection & Control Instrument Co. Ltd and Caoqian Xinyuan Company
2006
The Second Intermediate People's Court of Beijing

DISPUTE OVER EXCLUSIVE RIGHTS TO REGISTERED TRADEMARK

The Plaintiff holds the exclusive rights to the registered trademarks entitled "丹佛斯", "Danfoss" and "DANFOSS". The first Defendant, Zibo-based Danfosi Detection & Control Instrument Co. Ltd, used the logos of "danfosi", "丹佛斯" for the infringing products in its business activities, registered an Internet domain name of "danfosi.com" and used " 丹佛斯 " in the name of its enterprise. The second Defendant, Caoqian Xinyuan Company, was involved in sales of the above infringing products.

HELD: The registered trademarks "丹佛斯", "Danfoss" and "DANFOSS" owned by the Plaintiff have been sanctioned for application to products similar to the infringing pressure transmitter products that are the subject of the lawsuit. As the logo of "丹佛斯" used by the first Defendant, Zibo-based Danfosi Detection & Control Instrument Co. Ltd, is identical to the logo of "丹佛斯" to which the trademark rights are owned by the Plaintiff, the use of the identical logo is sufficient to cause public confusion and misunderstanding. Although the first Defendant claims that "danfosi" is the title in the Chinese phonetic alphabet for its enterprise name, it is highly similar to the logo of "DANFOSS" to which the exclusive trademark rights are owned by the Plaintiff and use of this logo is also sufficient to cause public confussion and misunderstanding. Consequently, the Defendant's actions shall be construed as infringements of the Plaintiff's exclusive right to use the trademark. The First Defendant Zibo-basd Danfosi Detection & Control Instrument Co. Ltd, shall cease producing and selling the infringing products immediately. The second Defendant, Caoqiao Xinyuan, which presented evidence of legitimate sourcing for the accused infringing products, may not be liable for compensation but it must stop selling the accused infringing products immediately.

As provided in Law, the registration of words identical or similar to another's trademark as a domain name, and the conduct of e-businesses at this domain, causing public misunderstanding, shall be construed as an act infringing the exclusive rights of a registered trademark.

CASE NO. 61

Cui Shixun Vs. Liaoning Provincial Library
2006
The Intermediate People's Court of Ha'erbin City, Heilongjiang Province

MORAL RIGHTS DISPUTE

In the book titled *United Bibliography of Thread-bound Ancient Books in Northeastern China*, the Defendant used the works of the Plaintiff but the book was not marked with the signature of the Plaintiff.

HELD: The Defendant's act violated the principle of fairness and good faith, and also infringed the Plaintiff's right of signature. The Defendant shall rectify its action by adding a correction page to copies of the book already printed and under distribution, and the Defendant shall also publish a statement of apology to the Plaintiff in relevant newspapers.

CASE NO. 62

Eastman Kodak Company Vs. Keda Elevator Company
2005
First Intermediate People's Court of Suzhou City Jiangsu Province

TRADEMARK INFRINGEMENT DISPUTE

The Plaintiff is the owner of the registered trademark "KODAK" and trademarks focusing on "KODAK" characters. Without permission the Defendant used identification separately or with "Keda" in upper and lower case to clearly designate "KODAK" on their elevator products, doorplate, and name cards for employees, product instructions and advertising documents. The Defendant and its Beijing branch have respectively made applications to China Internet Management Center for registration of "kodaklift.com.cn" and "kodak-bj.com" as domain names, to be used for Internet advertising operations.

HELD: The Plaintiff is a US-based company. Both China and the United States are members of the Paris Convention for the Protection of Industrial Property and the World Trade Organization, so that recorded judgments in this case should be in line with the relevant Laws of China and the Paris Convention for the Protection of Industrial Property as well as the General Agreement on Tariffs and the TRIPS Agreement on Trades (including trades among the counterfeit goods). The "KODAK" trademark of the Plaintiff holds a relatively high market reputation and is well known by the public, so it should be listed as a "famous trademark" and should hold the high level of protection approved by Law for merchandise or service fields. Without the permission of the Plaintiff, owner of "KODAK", the Defendant has used the "KODAK" trademark many times and in different ways and these actions should be judged as trademark infringements.

CHINESE COURT JUDGEMENTS: INTELLECTUAL PROPERTY

PART THREE: 1998 - 2003

CASE NO. 63

Autodesk Co. Ltd Vs. Longfa Co. Ltd
2003
Beijing No.2 Middle-level People's Court

COMPUTER SOFTWARE COPYRIGHT INFRINGEMENT DISPUTE

The Defendant, which is not approved by the Plaintiff to use the copyright it holds, randomly installed and used 155 sets of the Plaintiff's AutoCAD series and 3ds Max series software.

HELD: The Plaintiff has registered copyright in the United States of America for the five kinds of computer software that are the subject of the case, and its ownership of the copyright should be protected by Chinese Law. The Defendant is a professional enterprise, engaged in design and residential construction and in public architectural decoration, and is not approved by the Plaintiff to randomly copy, install the design software and the five kinds of architectural drawings to which the case refers, nor to use them in business nor to take the profits from their business usage. The actions of the Defendant described above, infringed the computer software copyright which the Plaintiff owns in Law.

CASE NO. 64

(America) Education Testing Service Center (ETS) Vs. New Oriental School
2003
Beijing Supreme People's Court

COPYRIGHT DISPUTE

The Plaintiff is the legal representative of the "TOEFL" brand (with the scope of verifying audio typing, testing services and publications etc, respectively). From 1989 to 1999, the Plaintiff developed 53 sets of TOEFL test questions for which it registered the copyright at the U.S. Copyright Office. The Defendant is not approved by the Plaintiff to copy and sell TOEFL test questions, within its teaching course.

HELD: By copying and selling the TOEFL test questions, the Defendant has infringed the Plaintiff's copyright and should therefore undertake the relevant legal responsibility. However, in view of the special character of TOEFL test questions and the special form and purpose for which the Defendant utilizes this work, explaining the test questions of TOEFL in class and in a context that did not use infringing documents which belong to the relevant works, the Defendant did not commit any other infringement to other copyright. Although the Plaintiff legally registered the TOEFL brand for video publication, the Defendant uses the "TOEFL" typeface prominently on "TOEFL series teaching courses" and "TOEFL magnetic audio tapes". However, the Defendant is using the brand for the description and illustration of "TOEFL", for which the only purpose is to specify and stress that the content of the publication relates to TOEFL testing, in order to make readers easily understand the content of the publication and in a way which is not present in the original of the publication. This usage cannot cause readers to be mistaken and confused as to the origin of the product. Therefore, the relevant actions of the Defendant do not violate the private brand rights of the Plaintiff.

CASE NO. 65

America Adobe Co. Ltd Vs. Shanghai Nianhua Computer Videotext Technology Co. Ltd
2000
Shanghai Supreme People's Court

COMPUTER SOFTWARE COPYRIGHT INFRINGEMENT DISPUTE

The Plaintiff is the copyright holder of "adobe typeset expert 6.5 version" software, "adobe electronic photo studio 5.0 version" software, and "adobe painting master 8.0 version" software. The Defendant randomly installs these software programs during the course of its computer sales and random gift software.

HELD: The Defendant is a professional distributor that trades in computers and computer products, and should know that there is no copyright approval for the use of computer software subject to copyright that anyone copies randomly and gives away; this defines the mistaken actions of the Defendant. Therefore, the Defendant's actions of copying and installing the Plaintiff's software in order to sell computers and for the purpose of making profits, infringes the computer software copyright belonging to the Plaintiff. The Defendant must undertake to cease its infringement, eliminate its promotion, apologize publicly and compensate for loss etc. under its civil responsibility, in accordance with the Law.

CASE NO. 66

Laolishi Co. Ltd Vs. Beijing Cinet Information Co. Ltd
2001
Beijing No.2 Middle-Level People's Court

BRAND INFRINGEMENT DISPUTE

"ROLEX" is the brand of the Plaintiff since 1992, and the Plaintiff has successively registered "ROLEX" multi-brands, on different kinds of commodities in China. The Plaintiff promotes its manufactured products widely, mainly "ROLEX" watches, since they are sold at the markets of the main cities in China. In 1999, the Plaintiff's "ROLEX" brand was listed in the National Key Brands Protection List by the State Administration for Industry and Commerce (SAIC). On May 5, 1999, the Defendant applied for registration of the generic name "ROLEX", which was not granted.

HELD: "ROLEX" is the well-known brand of the Plaintiff, to which the relevant rights and benefits should belong, and the Defendant has no justification for registering the "ROLEX" name as the name of is enterprise. The registered brand of the Plaintiff as its generic name was not truly used. The action demonstrating such an application of the brand was to apply for registration. The Defendant applied for registration of the brand as the name of its enterprise and thus its malicious intent is evident. The actions of the Defendant have no justification because relevant consumers mistakenly confuse the holder of the "ROLEX" field name with ownership of the "ROLEX" registered brand. Disruption in the business regulation of legal competition violates the basic principle of honesty and infringes on the civil legal rights of the Plaintiff. It is a form of unfair competition and should be subject to the relevant civil responsibility.

CASE NO. 67

Lek-Yuen Company Vs. Jinlanwan Company
2002
The Higher People's Court of Jiangsu Province

DISPUTE OVER COUNTERFEITING AND FORGING WELL-KNOWN PRODUCT-SPECIFIC NAMES, PACKAGING AND DECORATION

"Baijia Lake" is the name of a place that the Plaintiff applies as its registered trademark. The real estate developed by the Defendant is in the vicinity of Baijia Lake, and the Defendant uses "Baijia Lake" as the name of its real estate. The Plaintiff claims that the Defendant is infringing its exclusive trademark rights and demands that it ceases the infringement and compensates for loss.

HELD: The real estate development site of Jinlanwan Real Estate Development Co. Ltd. is not located in Baijia Lake, and there are a number of other development sites of other real estate companies between the Defendant's site and Baijia Lake; so the use of "Baijia Lake" by the Defendant in its advertisements and sales brochures for its commercial property is not a proper use, constituting an infringement of the exclusive trademark rights for "Baijia Lake" of the Plaintiff.

CASE NO. 68

Tianjin Quanxing Sporting Products Factory v. Sichuan Quanxing Football Club, Nanjing Sports Equipment Factory
2000
The Higher People's Court of Jiangsu Province

TRADEMARK INFRINGEMENT DISPUTE
The Plaintiff acquired the trademarks "Quanxing" and "Quanxing and map" by assignment. On November 21, 1996, the Defendants agreed to cooperate in the production of "97 Memorial Football", under which the second Defendant, Nanjing Sports Equipment Factory, had the right to use the first Defendant's 1997 Quanxing Club emblem, mascot, photographs and signatures of team players and coaches, as well as production and marketing rights. The football and basketball involved in the case produced by the second Defendant were marked respectively "Quanxing", "Sichuan Quanxing" or "Sichuan Quanxing Football Club" together with other words. When using the word "Quanxing" alone, the font is Traditional Chinese and the size is larger, being clearly prominent above other words.

HELD: The business brand "Quanxing" of the first Defendant, Sichuan Quanxing Club, is from "Quanxing" China Time-honored Brand of Sichuan Chengdu Quanxing Distillery, and it is a well-known national brand. The well-known brand itself has a high popularity and business reputation, so that it naturally causes a strong effect on advertising and public attraction and has a high commercial value; thus, a well-known brand is the intangible property of a commercial entity. The use by the first Defendant, Sichuan Quanxing Club, of the word "Quanxing" on the memorial and gift balls can be seen both as taking the identity and the use of its brand. Therefore, it is a legitimate and reasonable use of its business brand and not an act to extend inappropriately the scope of its use.

CASE NO. 69

Suzuki Motor Corporation Vs. San Li Company
2003
The Intermediate People's Court of Changsha City

TRADEMARK INFRINGEMENT DISPUTE
The Plaintiff is a leading global automobile and motorcycle manufacturing company, and its trademarks "SUZUKI" and "Lin Mu" have already been registered in China. Since then, the Plaintiff places its trademarks on the obvious parts of its automotive products, and the motorcycles and accessories it produces, which are well known by consumers. The Defendant placed the trademark "SUSIKI" on the obvious parts of its SK series of motorcycle products, which is similar to the plaintiff's trademark "SUZUKI", and the Defendant also describes its products directly as "Suzuki King" or "Suzuki Prince" throughout its sales and promotional materials.

HELD: Comprehensive judgement on the similarity of goods and trademarks should be based on the principle of whether they will cause confusion, combined with their significance and visibility, as well as the objective awareness of the registered trademarks by ordinary consumers. In this case, the Plaintiff's products cover automobiles and motorcycles, and it holds a positive reputation in the international market – its trademark has significance and visibility. The Defendant and its distributors, during their advertising and marketing processes, also use "Suzuki King" to promote their motorcycle products, drawing on the market advantage enjoyed by the Plaintiff in order to confuse normal consumers and cause them to misunderstand that the brand's origin is specifically related to the Plaintiff. After comparing objectively, it can be seen that the trademark "SUSIKI" used by the Defendant has no specific meaning and is similar to the Plaintiff's registered trademark "SUZUKI" in terms of shape, pronunciation and overall composition. The difference in visual appearance of the two is not significant, which is sufficient to cause consumer confusion.

Therefore, the Defendant's act of using the trademark "SUSIKI" on its motorcycle products constitutes an infringement of the Plaintiff's registered "SUZUKI" trademark.

CASE NO. 70

Lin Yi v. ChinaNews Agency
2001
The Higher People's Court of Beijing Municipality

DISPUTE OVER PROTECTION OF INTEGRITY RIGHTS

The Defendant, on the album cover that it publishes, uses the color photographic work *Jump to Help* shot by the Plaintiff to reflect the anti-smuggling activities of customs officers and the written words denigrate the work of customs officers in the photograph images.

HELD: The Plaintiff owns the copyright of his photographic work *Jump to Help* in accordance with the Law. The Defendant, without the Plaintiff's authorization, used the Plaintiff's photographs on the cover of the magazine that it edited and published, without the name of the Plaintiff and seriously distorting and changing the Plaintiff's intended meaning. Therefore, the Defendant should bear the infringement liability, cease the infringement, apologize publicly to the Plaintiff and pay compensation for loss.

CASE NO. 71

Beijing Finance City Network Co. Ltd v. Chengdu Moneywise Software Co. Ltd.
2000
Beijing Second Intermediate People's Court

UNFAIR COMPETITION DISPUTE

The Plaintiff has organized staff to conduct software development so as to process the instant quotation of foreign exchange transactions, and to publish the data in the form of foreign exchange graphs on its website. The Defendant on the Moneywise website that it has set up has created a direct link to the graphs of the foreign exchange center channel on the Plaintiff's website. Bypassing the homepage of the Plaintiff's Finance City website, the Defendant has directly linked the graphs to the foreign exchange center column of its Moneywise website, and, throughout the period of the linkage, did not revise the overall display state of the linked graphs.

HELD: The two Parties to this case are both website operators and there is a relationship of commercial competition between them. The Defendant, without the Plaintiff's permission, set up unauthorized direct links to the contents of the sub-pages under the homepage of the Plaintiff's website. Such an action is contrary to the interests of the Plaintiff and should be regarded as unfair competition.

CASE NO. 72

Xinhai Advertising Company v. Chengdu Economic TV Station
1998
Intermediate People's Court of Chengdu City, Sichuan Province

COPYRIGHT DISPUTE

The Defendant continues to transmit a TV program to which the exclusive telecast rights are owned by others after the expiry of its televising rights. The Plaintiff believes that the Defendant's aforesaid action is a violation of its legal rights and interests, so brings its suit to the Court.

HELD: The exclusive telecast rights acquired by the Plaintiff through paid transfer should be protected by Law. The Plaintiff and the Defendant signed an agreement for the Defendant to televise *Destiny's Child Prodigy* once only, but the Defendant televised it again without the Plaintiff's permission. Such an act violates the radio telecast rights of the Plaintiff in the Chengdu region.

CASE NO. 73

Jiang Haixin v. Philips Company
2002
Shanghai No.2 Intermediate People's Court

TRADEMARK INFRINGEMENT DISPUTE
The Plaintiff has registered the domain name "philipscis.com" and opened a corresponding English language website with this domain name. The Defendant considered that the Plaintiff's act constituted a violation of its exclusive trademark rights. Therefore it applied for arbitration to WIPO Arbitration and Mediation Center. On September 19, 2002, WIPO Arbitration and Mediation Center gave a ruling on the applicant Philips Company's complaint: the disputed domain name philipscis.com should be transferred to the applicant. The Plaintiff refused to accept the aforesaid decision and then filed its suit to the Court.

HELD: The trademark "PHILIPS" of the Defendant has already been registered in China, and it is protected by Chinese Law. For the domain name philipscis.com registered by the Plaintiff, the first seven letters ("philips") are the same as the Defendant's PHILIPS trademark, and the last three letters "cis" are similar to the acronym for the Defendant's sub-department "CSI", only in a different order. Therefore, it should be acknowledged that this domain name is similar to the trademark of the Defendant and sufficient to cause misunderstanding by the relevant public. Taking together the domain name registered and its usage by the Plaintiff, it should be recognized that the Plaintiff's purpose in registering the domain name was to use the Defendant's popularity to mislead and attract internet users to visit its website of this domain name, and that the Plaintiff maliciously violated the Defendant's legitimate rights and interests.

CASE NO. 74

Music Copyright Society of China v. NetEase.com, Inc. and China Mobil Ltd.
2002
Beijing Second Intermediate People's Court

COPYRIGHT DISPUTE

The Plaintiff is the manager of the song *Glory of Blood*, and according to an agreement with the author, the Plaintiff owns the management rights to upload, download and transfer this music onto the Internet. The first Defendant, NetEase.com, Inc, without the permission of the composer, Su Yue, or the Plaintiff and without any payment, provides a download service for *Glory of Blood* to users on its website. The second Defendant, China Mobil Ltd, provides paid services to users for processing the aforesaid download.

HELD: The first Defendant, NetEase.com, Inc, collects and publicly displays the music *Glory of Blood* on pages of its website directly without permission, and provides paid download services to users of China Mobil Ltd; this act constitutes a violation of the information network dissemination rights of the copyright holder. Therefore, the first Defendant shall bear civil liability for ceasing the infringement and compensating for loss. The second Defendant, China Mobil Ltd, provides a paid infrastructure service, which is a legitimate and lawful business practice not constituting a violation of copyright of the song *Glory of Blood*.

CASE NO. 75

Japanese Yamaha v. South Motorcycle Corporation Limited and Gangtian Co. Ltd
2002
The Higher People's Court of Tianjin

TRADEMARK INFRINGEMENT DISPUTE

The registered trademarks of "YAMAHA" and "VISION" are the property of the Plaintiff. The first Defendant, South Motorcycle Corporation Limited, sold motors labeled "Licensed by YAMAHA". The Second Defendant, Gangtian Co. Ltd, posted transparent stickers marked with the words "engine licensed by YAMAHA" on the front and back sections of motorcycles they produced. The Plaintiff maintained that both the above Defendants' acts infringed its exclusive user rights to the trademark, and filed its suit to the Court.

HELD: Fluctuation in sales volume can be influenced by many factors in the market; the trademark infringement of the Defendants is not an unique factor, and that is why the Court believes that the influences of the Defendants' infringement of trademark on the sales volume of the Plaintiff's joint venture cannot be used as direct evidence for compensation claims. It is difficult to determine a reasonable amount for costs of the Plaintiff's lawsuit based on the information provided by the Plaintiff. With regard to advertising costs, items are included that bear no relation to this lawsuit. However, the Plaintiff's reasonable assertions about the extent of the compensation will be considered in determining the amount of compensation levied on the two Defendants. Whereas the amount of loss arising from the Defendants' infringement in this case is difficult to determine and is subject to the provisions in "Principles on Compensation for Infringement of Rights" and the "Principle of Fairness and Good Faith in General Principles" of the Civil Law of the People's Republic of China, the reasonable factors for compensation and the relevant circumstances will be considered properly in determining compensation.

CASE NO. 76

Xuzhou Handu Industrial Development Co. Ltd Vs. Japanese Olympus Optical Industry Co.
2000
The Higher People's Court of Beijing

TRADEMARK INFRINGEMENT DISPUTE

The Plaintiff is the exclusive rights owner of the text trademark of "千禧龙QIANXILONG". The Defendant, without the Plaintiff's permission, printed the Chinese characters of "千禧龙", similar to the Plaintiff's trademark of "千禧龙 QIANXILONG" in prominent places such as the camera body, package box and credit card for the Olympus WIDE80 camera produced by the Defendant and marketed in all large cities across China.

HELD: Although the Defendant used a traditional Chinese word for its camera, the word is still the same word used in the Plaintiff's trademark, and such wording is sufficient to cause consumer misunderstanding and shall be construed as an infringement of the exclusive registered trademark rights of the Plaintiff. The Defendant shall be liable for compensation.

CASE NO. 77

DuPont Vs. Beijing Guowang Information Co. Ltd
2000
The Higher People's Court of Beijing

TRADEMARK INFRINGEMENT DISPUTE

The USA-based Plaintiff acquired the proprietary rights to the trademark of "DuPont" in elliptical font by assignment. Since 1992, the Plaintiff has invested huge sums in advertising across China and in publicizing the "DuPont" trademark in elliptic font in multiple ways, and this trademark is now highly popular in China. The Defendant registered the domain name of "dupont.com.cn" with the CNNIC (China Internet Network Information Center) and this domain has not been put to use until now.

HELD: Without legal rights, the Defendant clearly gains commercial benefits from the famous trademark of DuPont which belongs to the Plaintiff. The Defendant's act violated the principle of good faith, infringed the Plaintiff's exclusive user rights to the DuPont trademark and also constituted illicit competition with the Plaintiff. Therefore, the Defendant shall accept the appropriate civil liability.

CASE NO. 78

Inter Ikea Systems B.V. Vs Beijing Guowang Information Co. Ltd
2000
The Higher People's Court of Beijing

TRADEMARK INFRINGEMENT DISPUTE

The Plaintiff is the owner of the "IKEA" trademark and the associated trademark for the "IKEA" design, as well as the trademark of "千禧龙". The Defendant applied for the domain name of "ikea.com.cn" with CNNIC (China Internet Network Information Center) which it did not put into network operation.

HELD: Having no legal rights, the Defendant clearly gains commercial benefits from the Plaintiff's famous trademark which should belong to the Plaintiff. The Defendant's act violates the principle of good faith, infringes the exclusive trademark user rights of the Plaintiff and also constitutes illicit competition with the Plaintiff. Therefore, the Defendant shall accept the appropriate civil liability.

CASE NO. 79

Zhao Jikang Vs. Qujing Cigarette Factory
2003
The Higher People's Court of Yunnan Province

LITERARY PROPERTY DISPUTE

The Plaintiff and his peer Wang Gongpu jointly created the film script of *Five Golden Flowers* by assignment. In 1983, the Defendant applied for registration of *Five Golden Flowers* as a cigarette trademark with the State Trademark Bureau. Today, "Five Golden Flowers" branded cigarettes are still in production and on sale. The Plaintiff claims that, without permission from the two authors, the Defendant arbitrarily used the Five Golden Flowers as a trademark for its cigarettes, makes money from the popularity of *Five Golden Flowers*, seriously harmed the prior interests of the Plaintiff and Wang Gongpu to create the film work of *Five Golden Flowers*, infringed their literary rights and this action constitutes unfair competition.

HELD: The Plaintiff and his peer own the literary rights to the film script of *Five Golden Flowers*, so that the Plaintiff can apply to the Court for protection of their legal benefits within the period of copyright protection. However, there is an insufficient legal basis for the Plaintiff's claim for copyright protection of the work title in accordance with the applicable Copyright Law and the claim is untenable. The Defendant's action cannot be construed as unfair competition.

CASE NO. 80

Anhui Xiaoxiao Technology Industrial Co. Ltd Vs. Jixi County Light Chain Factory
2000
The Supreme People's Court

TRADE SECRET INFRINGEMENT DISPUTE

The Plaintiff protects its chain processing technology as trade secrets. Co-Defendants B and C had worked for the Plaintiff before going to work for the Defendanty. The Plaintiff claimed that the Defendant used its technical secrets and customer lists, divulged by B and C, to manufacture and trade in chain products.

HELD: The five technical features in question include a four-step mold formed at one time by the Plaintiff, which has become common technology in the public domain, and the sleeve roll mold of the Defendant was developed by that factory itself. Therefore, the Plaintiff's claim that the Defendant and Co-Defendants B and C have violated its sleeve roll mold technology secrets cannot be established.

Lightning Source UK Ltd.
Milton Keynes UK
UKOW02f2128290916

284131UK00002B/430/P

9 781907 461200